Books by Charles W. Yost

The Age of Triumph and Frustration:
  Modern Dialogues
The Insecurity of Nations
The Conduct and Misconduct of Foreign Affairs

The
Conduct
and
Misconduct
of
Foreign Affairs

The Conduct and Misconduct of Foreign Affairs

CHARLES W. YOST

Random House   New York

Library of Congress Cataloging in Publication Data

Yost, Charles Woodruff.
   The conduct and misconduct of foreign affairs.

   Includes bibliographical references.
    1.   International relations. 2.   United States—
Foreign relations—20th century. I.   Title.
JX1391.Y68   327.73   72-4818
ISBN 0-394-47373-6

To Irena
who shared with unfailing zest my
thirty-five years of foreign affairs

With love and gratitude

The central question, as I see it, is whether the wonderfully diverse and gifted assemblage of human beings on this earth really knows how to run a civilization.

Survival is still an open question, not because of environmental hazards but because of the workings of the human mind. And day by day the problem grows more complex.

It was recognized clearly and with compassion by Pope John; to him the human race was not a cold abstraction. Underlying his messages and encyclicals was this simple thought: that the human race is a family, that men are brothers, all wars are civil wars, and all killing is fratricidal.

—Adlai Stevenson
"Pacem in Terris" Convocation, February 1965

Acknowledgments

I should like to make two acknowledgments for indispensable assistance in the preparation of this book.

The first is to Maureen Corr who painstakingly did much of the necessary research, who faultlessly transcribed long series of drafts and redrafts and who, most important of all, maintained even on the most hectic of days the atmosphere of calm and good humor so essential to creativity. I am eternally grateful to her.

The second acknowledgment is to all my colleagues and associates at the United Nations, and particularly the U.S. Mission to the UN, during the years 1961 to 1966 and again from 1969 to 1971. Thanks to their harmonious common efforts I became convinced that it is more and more possible to conduct the foreign affairs of a community of nations jointly in and through international institutions rather than separately and competitively under the traditional panoplies of power.

March 23, 1972   C.W.Y.

Contents

Introduction

In a biography of Louis XI,* the monarch who at the end of the Middle Ages brutally but decisively hammered together the French nation out of its feudal components, Paul Kendall described as follows the contemporaneous but very different state of affairs on the Italian peninsula:

> In the world of Italian interstate relations, Louis well knew, everything was magnified. The smallest gesture, subjected to elaborate analysis, became a menace; the slightest fortuity, studied with unrelenting minuteness, was turned into a dangerous portent. The face of Italian politics was scrutinized at claustrophobically close range: the twitch of a cheek, tremor of a lip, a slide of eyeball assumed significance, probably sinister. Excellent communications, the most elaborate network of diplomats and secret agents the world had ever seen, often served to darken rather than promote understanding. Packed tightly into an intensely

*Paul Kendall, *Louis XI: the Universal Spider* (New York: W. W. Norton, 1970).

competitive political space, the five great powers of the peninsula—Venice, Milan, Florence, the Papacy, and the Kingdom of Naples—to whom were joined in varying degrees of political symbiosis a dozen minor states, constantly shifted policies and alliances in a stylized ballet that was brilliantly energized by the magnetic field of their mutual suspicions. Within this closed space statecraft had become capable of every-thing but statesmanship; subtlety of calculation, able master all political mathematics except harmony.

Plus ça change, plus c'est la même chose. The world is both larger and smaller than it was in the fifteenth century. The global great powers of the 1970's are, almost more than their Italian counterparts five hundred years before, "packed tightly into an intensely competitive political space," and still all too often "within this closed space statecraft becomes capable of everything but statesman-ship." Half a millennium's experience with international diplomacy, three centuries' exposure to science—two to rationalism and democracy and one to ever-more rapid transport and communication—have not yet taught the governments of nation-states the "mathematics of har-mony," or even of "peaceful coexistence."

Questions are often raised these days about the rele-vance of the past, not only the Middle Ages but the 1940's and 1950's. Of course, political conceptions or stereotypes which were relevant to another time, if carried over uncrit-ically to this one, may prove inapplicable, distorting, even disastrous. That sort of past is much better dead.

The relevance of history, however, as of all human experience, is to help avoid present and future mistakes by testing not only what did and did not work in the past, but also whether that which worked not long ago may already be obsolete and that which has only just been perceived may already have become indispensable. Like every other manifestation of human wisdom and human folly, foreign policy needs to be fundamentally reexamined every few years, not merely in light of the fads and follies of the present, which are no better than those of the past, but in the light of sober judgment about what in fact helps and what hinders the struggle for international harmony today.

The purpose of this book will be to shed some light on the melancholy paradox that while man's knowledge and capacities have expanded so enormously, his conduct of relations among his chosen political entities, the nation-states, remains almost as primitive, unsophisticated and irrational as it was at the end of the Middle Ages.

The book begins with a few brief vignettes of some critical moments, to which the author happened to be eyewitness, in the history of the last forty years—glimpses designed to convey an impression of both the climate and the incoherence of that period. There follows an inventory, also brief and without evaluation, of the traditional and still prevailing objects of foreign policy and of the new conditions to which policy will have to adapt.

The main body of the book will be an account of the conduct and misconduct of foreign affairs by modern governments, particularly that of the United States—once again illustrated from the author's experience. This account will include a close look at the present instruments of foreign policy, to see where they have failed and how they might be better adapted to pursuing rational and relevant objects.

The book concludes with an examination of what must soon become, in light of the changes transforming human existence, the new and essential objects of foreign policy, as distinguished from those chimerical objects which destroyed the Greek and Italian city-states so long ago, and some modern states so recently. How to make the transition from old to new objects, from old to new instruments, is explored. My ultimate conclusion, however, is that the conduct of foreign affairs in the modern world probably cannot become rational until these affairs cease to be "foreign"—until the interests of the world community, of the small world the astronauts observe from their spacecraft, are seen both to outweigh and to comprise the interests of each nation-state.

The
Conduct
and
Misconduct
of
Foreign Affairs

Eyewitness to Endings and Beginnings

Paris: March 26, 1929   The students have been waiting since dawn in the mist.
They perch on the stone rail-
ings around the Place de la Concorde; they pull up chairs
to the curbstone of the Elysian Fields and sit there eating
rolls; they climb to the roof of the Museum of the Tennis
Court and see the people of Paris flowing silently down all
the streets.

It is the funeral of Marshal Ferdinand Foch, the victor
of the greatest war in history. From the Marne he reported
to Paris: "My right is annihilated; my center is broken in
pieces; am attacking with my left; situation excellent."
Four years later, commander of all the armies of the Allies,
he sat in the railway car at Compiègne, watching with cold
eyes as the Germans signed their capitulation.

Now his armies are marching for the last time in his
honor, from Notre Dame to the Invalides. The British in
red, Scotsmen kilted, the Prince of Wales under an enor-

mous busby, staggering a little, sweat on his brow; the Belgians, the Americans, the Italian chasseurs, the tremendous Poles, the Serbs, the Japanese, the Portuguese; then the French themselves, the poilus riding the guns, the spahis in long cream-colored robes on white prancing horses, the black Senegalese, the small pale Vietnamese.

A cannon booms. A little figure walking alone, a red ribbon across his breast, a silk hat on his head: the President of the Republic. A line of old men, bareheaded, Poincaré with beard jutting, shaggy-haired Briand with hunched shoulders, Tardieu spruce and cold, Loucheur hollow-eyed. Many of them had been his enemies; now they march. The representatives of two score nations, Paderewski for Poland, Myron Herrick for the United States. The *anciens combatants* of France; four men leading who show no faces—contorted pits where features were; blind men groping, gripping a comrade's arm; young men struggling on wooden legs or armless; all proudly keeping step under the forest of flags. Once again the cannon. A pause. Silence.

One soldier is leading a horse without a rider. Its hoofs beat upon the street, at times it starts and stares about, affrighted. The gun carriage follows. Beside it the commanders of the armies: Pershing, the marshals of France—Lyautey, Franchet d'Esperey, Pétain. On the coffin a flag, a sword and one bare wreath. Again the cannon, muffled in the mist.

In only eleven years emissaries of Marshal Pétain, the victor of Verdun, will be signing in the same railway car in Compiègne the capitulation of France. Hitler will be doing his little dance of triumph, Mussolini will be stabbing his neighbor in the back, and the Japanese will be occupying a remote obscure possession of France called Vietnam.

Où sont les neiges d'antan?

Geneva: September 1929 The tenth anniversary, the high-water mark of the League of Nations. The students have come to learn, admire and wonder. One afternoon they meet Lord Robert Cecil, immensely tall and lean, glowing benevolently, bending toward them ingratiatingly, one of the fathers of the League, proud of his progeny, incurably hopeful; and Lady Astor, pert, incisive, indefatigable, youthful, daughter of Virginia in the House of Commons, unwitting grandmother of Women's Lib.

The students sit in the Assembly Hall of the Palais des Nations, listening to the great men of Europe's revival and reconciliation—Ramsay MacDonald, Aristide Briand, Gustav Stresemann.

MacDonald, handsome, evangelistic, the Scottish prophet. "The prospect before the present session of the Assembly," he intones, "is a happy, hopeful and an encouraging one. We are met here as Members of the League, in the spirit of the League, and with unruffled friendship and unreserved cooperation . . . Let us remember that the peoples of the whole world ask us to go forward, that the peoples of every nation desire us to act quickly because they want to close forever the old military chapters of Europe . . . My Government would urge the [Disarmament] Commissions not to face their problems from the point of view of the possibility of war . . . It would urge them to face them on the assumption that the risk of war breaking out now is far less than the hope of permanent peace. We have to ask our military advisers to remember that there is just as much security in a political agreement as there is in a regiment of soldiers, or in a fleet of battleships . . ."

And Briand, shaggy, supple, ironic, his shapeless jacket flapping loosely, his small hands plucking visions from the air, the most subtle eloquence this student has ever heard. The League, he says, "enjoys universal confidence and has built up a moral capital which is without parallel in the history of the world. But at this point a serious problem arises. What use is the League going to make of this trust which the nations have placed in it? . . . Yes, despite the League's efforts in the cause of peace, one serious omission exists which sooner or later we must remedy. We have agreed to place a ban on war; war henceforth will be deemed a crime. . . . Now, at last, we have our enemy by the throat; now we have him fast in the pillory. That is all to the good . . . But who would venture to say that this is enough? . . . No, gentlemen, not until the League, having condemned the crime, has taken such precautions as lie within its power to prevent that crime from being committed, or to punish it when committed—not until then will it have completed its duty."

And Stresemann, shaven of head and jowl, parchment-yellow, emaciated, the wisest and boldest leader of the Weimar Republic, the shadow of death already upon him. "I think I may now say that not only Germany and the occupying Powers but the League itself must rejoice that the early evacuation of Germany by foreign troops was definitely decided upon last week. In this connection I would recall the noble words of the British Prime Minister spoken from this platform: 'A political agreement offers as much security as regiments of soldiers.' If this barrier which has separated Germany from her Western neighbors since the Armistice is broken down, the way will be cleared for that close and fruitful collaboration between Germany and her former adversaries which is so necessary in the interests of all nations, and consequently of the League itself."

Just one month later Stresemann will be dead, and in less than three years Briand, broken-hearted, who dreamed too soon—or too late—of a united Europe. In two years the Japanese will walk out of the Palais des Nations, in six

*years the Nazis and the Fascists, and from that platform
will be heard for the last time the high-pitched, reedy,
bitter voice of Haile Selassie, Lion of Judah, King of
Kings.*

Berlin: November 1933   A   mournful   rain-drenched
                                   Central   European   autumn.
                                   Hitler has been in power ten
months and the leaves are falling from the lindens.

The visitor from America meets secretly in a shabby flat
with two Social Democrats who live underground clan-
destinely, writing pamphlets and listening for the knock
on the door. (One will later die in exile in America and the
other teach at the Free University of Berlin.) He attends
mass rallies in the Sportpalast, where Hitler and Goebbels
speak, the hoarse interminable pounding voices rising to
manic crescendo, the glistening sea of well-nourished
faces, delirious eyes, sweat of good German bodies, the
great, repeated, responsive, relentless roar: *"Sieg heil! Sieg
heil! Sieg heil!"*

On one such occasion, Hitler says: "The National So-
cialist State has once more planted in the minds of the
German people the thought that there is something higher
than the freedom of the individual; that is the freedom and
the life of all. This view must be maintained in all circumstances, by force if necessary. It is the task of the leaders to
recognize what is necessary for the nation and to carry that
through with iron resolution. . . . Whenever anyone casts
in my teeth the question, However did *you* come to create
a Movement like this? my answer is, I believe there is only
one man who at that time had the right to do so and he was
the soldier of the front line. The soldier had taken his skin
to market, not for the victory of this or that particular
view—for that end not a single man fell—but that this
German people might once more have faith in its own
future."

"Faith in its own future?" For Hitler, Goebbels and the brown-shirted audience in the Sportpalast the "thousand-year Reich" lasted twelve years. As for the two Social Democrats of the Resistance, one died in exile in America, and the other, a professor at the Free University of Berlin, has been labeled a "reactionary" by Maoist students and no longer holds classes in this city where he once risked his life for freedom.

Berlin–Potsdam:
July–August 1945

The American delegation, before the Potsdam Conference convenes, tours Berlin, a blackened, stinking, gruesome skeleton of a city. In front of the ruins of Kaiser Wilhelm's palace at the end of Unter den Linden there flourishes a macabre black market, a scene out of Breughel: blond boyish Russian soldiers and the tattered, dead-eyed women of Berlin, old and young, bartering cigarettes and Spam for watches, jewelry, porcelain horses or a quick turn in bed.

Through the silent pitted streets comes an endless procession, filthy, bone-weary, apathetic, dragging on makeshift wooden carts a jumble of household possessions or a grandmother or an old dog—refugees from the East, going they know not where. The marble halls of Hitler's Chancellery are blasted open to the sky, bare of everything but rubble, and in one room cheap medals lie ankle-deep; the dark caved-in cellars where he died smell of corpses and excrement. On a square before the shattered façade of a baroque palace, a haggard old woman shakes her fist at the Americans. "See what you've done, you pigs!" "And what did you do," one answers, "in Warsaw and Rotterdam and London?" Her pinched face is blank; her world does not extend beyond her own dead city.

In the intact and sumptuous Cecilienhof in Potsdam, surrounded by parks and Soviet troops with Tommy guns slung under their arms, sit the victorious Big Three, deciding the fate of the world. Truman, alert, bouncy, perched on the tip of his spine, masking the fearful novelty of his power with a style of breezy didactic assurance. Churchill, sunk deep in his chair, his pink baby face stuck onto his hunched shoulders, his voice high-pitched and querulous, body worn out from six years of world-wide war, but sense of history undimmed. Stalin, impeccable in a simple uniform, blowing cigarette smoke musingly to the ceiling, heavy features impassive, hooded eyes missing no slightest move, no "twitch of cheek, tremor of lip, slide of eyeball," certainly the shrewdest, most cunning of the three. Beside them Byrnes, Leahy, Attlee, Eden, Molotov, Vishinsky.

Truman is impatient at Churchill's long harangues about the past and the future; he cuts him off sharply; he wants to get home to finish the war with Japan. Churchill is off to London to preside over the election returns; he'll be back in two days, he says—but it is Attlee and Bevin who come back. Stalin is in no hurry; he is genial, conciliatory, quite willing to concede all the nonessentials; he sits impassively watching the smoke of his cigarette drift up and away. He rises from his chair only twice during the conference: once to shake the hand of Field Marshal Alexander, victor in Italy; once to walk around the table with a great map in his hand to show Truman what the boundaries of the new Poland will be.

The published *Protocol of Proceedings of the Conference* had this to say about Poland: "We have taken note with pleasure of the agreement reached among representative Poles from Poland and abroad which has made possible the formation, in accordance with the decisions reached at the Crimea Conference, of a Polish Provisional Government of National Unity recognized by the three powers. . . . The three powers note that the Polish Provisional Government of National Unity, in accordance with the decisions of the Crimea Conference, has agreed to the holding of free and unfettered elections as soon as possible on the basis of universal suffrage and secret ballot, in which all democratic and anti-Nazi parties shall have the right to take part and to put forward candidates, and that representatives of the Allied press shall enjoy full freedom to report to the world upon developments in Poland before and during elections."

A year after Potsdam, Churchill made his Fulton speech, proclaiming the ringing down of the Iron Curtain between East and West. A year later Truman gave his name to a doctrine which was echoed after a decade and a half by John Fitzgerald Kennedy. Meanwhile many elections have been held in Poland and her neighbors, but not one could conceivably be called "free and unfettered."

Prague: July 1947   A Fourth of July party in the gardens of the American ambassador, in the shadow of the Hradčany, the castle of Golden Prague that has seen so much history. Bright sunshine, hot. Everyone is there: the diplomatic corps, the elite of liberated Czechoslovakia, the members of the coalition government, deriving from the election the year before in which non-Communist parties won 62 percent of the vote. The government has publicly made known that it would accept an invitation to the first Marshall Plan meeting in Paris. The Poles have privately said they also would accept, but publicly they have been silent.

A whisper passes from mouth to mouth around the garden. Some members of the government are not here: Gottwald, the Communist Prime Minister, Masaryk, the Foreign Minister, Drtina, the staunchly pro-Western Minister of Justice. They are in Moscow, summoned by Stalin. An official statement has been issued there: Czechoslovakia has withdrawn its acceptance of the invitation to Paris. It was all an imperialist plot. Gottwald, Masaryk and Drtina have been tongue-lashed unmercifully by Stalin himself, like disobedient boys.

The garden party in the July sunshine buzzes like a swarm of bees. Diplomats and liberated Czechs take each other away from the crowd, behind a lilac bush, beyond the splashing fountain. What does it mean? What does that devious implacable man in the Kremlin have in mind? What will happen to Czechoslovakia? What will happen to us? Is it a beginning or an end?

Eight months later Jan Masaryk, son of Thomas, father of his country, is flung from a window of his apartment in the Czernin palace to the cobblestones below. Drtina breaks away from his interrogators and leaps from a window to his death. Their spirit lives, however, and lest it triumph, Soviet tanks have to move again after twenty years into golden Prague.

Washington:
June 25, 1950
At three o'clock in the morning, the phone rings in my bedroom. Dean Rusk, Assistant Secretary of State for the Far East, voice calm and controlled, wants the Director of Eastern European Affairs to know that the North Koreans have invaded South Korea.

Later in the morning the office of the Secretary of State, Dean Acheson, a solemn-faced conclave: the Secretary; Frank Pace, Secretary of the Army; Lawton Collins, Chief of Staff of the Army; Phillip Jessup, Ambassador at Large; Dean Rusk; Freeman Matthews, Deputy Undersecretary of State; John Hickerson, Assistant Secretary for United Nations Affairs; and a dozen others. No one has foreseen this; no one is quite sure what it means. There have been many other attempts since Potsdam, some successful, to extend the Communist empire by pressure, threats, coups or guerrilla war—all the countries in Eastern Europe occupied by Soviet armies, civil war in Greece, the Berlin blockade, the coup in Prague, the war of "liberation" in Vietnam—but this is the first direct aggression, the first overt hostile movement of armies across frontiers since the war ended. It could not conceivably have been undertaken by North Korea on its own; Moscow and Peking must have planned and wanted the attack. What does it portend? Will the Communist armies move across other frontiers in Asia, in Europe, elsewhere?

It seems clear to those gathered in Secretary Acheson's office this bright Sunday morning—many of them the same men who had by might and main shored up a tottering world over the past four years with the Truman Doctrine, the Marshall Plan, NATO—that this *will* happen, that the whole edifice from Japan to Greece, Turkey and Yugoslavia, even to Germany, Austria and beyond, will crumble and fall apart if the United States, with whatever power necessary and without losing an instant's time, does not move. And if the United Nations does not move too, it will suffer the fate of the League; it must thwart and punish the crime when committed, and "not until then will it have completed its duty."

The next day President Truman issues a statement which reads in part: "I conferred Sunday evening with the Secretaries of State and Defense, their senior advisers, and the Joint Chiefs of Staff about the situation in the Far East created by unprovoked aggression against the Republic of Korea. The Government of the United States is pleased with the speed and determination with which the UN Security Council acted to order a withdrawal of the invading forces to positions north of the 38th parallel. In accordance with the resolution of the Security Council, the United States will vigorously support the effort of the Council to terminate this serious breach of the peace. . . . Those responsible for this act of aggression must realize how seriously the Government of the United States views such threats to the peace of the world. Willful disregard of the obligation to keep the peace cannot be tolerated by nations that support the UN Charter."

The American people and the United Nations rally behind them. This is their finest hour. In three years the red tide in Korea is stemmed. And if later it floods southward—toward Indochina, for example—must it not, can it not, be stemmed in the same way? The United States has never been stronger and never lost a war.

Vientiane, Laos:
February 1955

The Crown Prince of Laos is giving a dinner for the American Secretary of State, John Foster Dulles, in the Royal Palace in Vientiane, a bare, drafty mansion through which the swallows fly; until a few months ago it was the French High Commissioner's residence. The lights are dim because Vientiane's antique power plant barely functions; through the paneless windows one can see only the shadows of great flame trees in the tropic night.

The Crown Prince, with his almost Chinese features and impassivity, is urbane and gracious as ever. He has with him the ministers of his new government, a coalition of all the non-Communist parties: the Prime Minister, Kataj, a little fighting cock; the bland Foreign Minister, Phoui Sananikone; and the Minister of Defense, erstwhile Prime Minister, who last year—to the grave dissatisfaction of the Crown Prince—negotiated the Geneva Accord for Laos, Prince Souvanna Phouma. Beside Dulles is Walter Robertson, Assistant Secretary for the Far East, a courtly, mellifluous Virginian, a single-minded and implacable enemy of Communism and of all coalition governments tainted with diversity and ambivalence. There is also present the entire diplomatic corps—that is, the French, British, American and Thai ambassadors.

Secretary Dulles is responding to the Crown Prince's toast with a timely but, at least as far as the British and

French ambassadors are concerned, unexpected little speech. A large part of the two northern provinces of Laos—Sam Neua and Phong Saly—he notes, are, seven months after the Geneva Accord, still militarily occupied by the Communist Pathet Lao and their North Vietnamese allies. The presence of North Vietnamese "foreign military forces" is in direct violation of the Accord; the Pathet Lao, who number only a couple of thousand, were permitted by the Accord to "regroup" in those provinces pending their "reintegration" into the national community, but they show no disposition to reintegrate and every disposition, abetted and reinforced by the North Vietnamese, to hold the provinces indefinitely as their private domain. The leaders of the Laotian government have told Mr. Dulles that they consider this situation intolerable. If the necessary arms can be promptly supplied by the United States, which a month ago took over from France the responsibility of maintaining the Laotian armed forces, the Laotian government will undertake to clear out this abscess of domestic rebellion and foreign intervention. This seems to Mr. Dulles a sound decision and an eminently reasonable request; the United States will be happy to comply with it. He raises his glass to the health of His Majesty the King of Laos.

The next morning the Secretary of State and his party are off to meet with other friends in the neighborhood: Prince Sihanouk of Cambodia and Prime Minister Diem of South Vietnam. The French and British ambassadors, after consulting their governments, inform the Crown Prince and his ministers in no uncertain terms that their governments take an extremely dim view of any resumption of hostilities in northern Laos, even to rectify violations of the Geneva Accords; and that, if the royal Laotian government should undertake such action, the French and British governments would withdraw from it all support. Even though the support they are receiving from France and Britain is negligible, the Laotians, a sweet-natured, unassuming people, are not used to ignoring the wishes of great powers. They abandon their plans for retrieving Sam Neua and Phong Saly by military action. Suspecting the die has been cast and lost, the Crown Prince retires disheartened to the mountain fastness of Luang Prabang.

Five years later the North Vietnamese and the Pathet Lao, profiting from internecine squabbles among the Lao majority, seize by force another large slice of Laos. Fifteen years later, they have occupied half the country and made it an active theater of the Vietnam war.

However, years after Dulles and Robertson have passed from the scene, after a dizzy succession of American, French and British ambassadors have come and gone, the Crown Prince, now King, remains in his royal capital of Luang Prabang, and Prince Souvanna Phouma is the immortal and indispensable Prime Minister of a coalition government.

United Nations, New York: October 1962   The Security Council is meeting in emergency session. Every seat on the floor around the table is taken, and diplomats from a hundred nations line the walls. The galleries are packed. The gavel falls; the great chamber is silent.

It is the most fateful crisis since 1945. Nuclear war can break out in days—or even hours. American reconnaissance planes have determined that over a period of several weeks the Soviets have been installing in Cuba nuclear rockets with a range of two thousand miles, capable of blanketing more than half of the United States and much of Latin America. President Kennedy has demanded the immediate removal of the missiles and demolition of the sites, has imposed a naval blockade or quarantine on Cuba and on Soviet vessels sailing toward it, has placed all U.S. forces on a high state of alert, and has brought the issue immediately before the Organization of American States and the United Nations.

Valerian Zorin of the Soviet Union, graying, shark-jawed, gold-toothed, one-time organizer of the 1948 coup in Prague, is in the chair of the Security Council this month. The U.S. representative is Adlai Stevenson, the eloquent liberal and humanitarian, long-time advocate of détente and reconciliation with the Soviet Union, all the more outraged therefore at what seems to him inexcusable deceit, treachery and violence. For once he speaks with the voice of passion.

"One of the sites, as I have said, was constructed in twenty-four hours. One of these missiles can be armed with its nuclear warhead in the middle of the night, pointed at New York, and landed above this room five minutes after it was fired. No debate in this room could affect in the slightest the urgency of these terrible facts or the immediacy of the threat to peace. . . .

"I have often wondered what the world would be like today if the situation at the end of the war had been reversed—if the United States had been ravaged and shattered by war, and if the Soviet Union had emerged intact in exclusive possession of the atomic bomb and overwhelming military and economic might. Would it have followed the same path and devoted itself to realizing the world of the Charter?

"Has the Soviet Union ever really joined the United Nations? Or does its philosophy of history and its conception of the future run counter to the pluralistic concept of this Charter? . . .

"I regret that people here at the United Nations seem to believe that the cold war is a private struggle between two great super-Powers. It is not a private struggle; it is a world civil war—a contest between the pluralistic world and the monolithic world—a contest between the world of the Charter and the world of communist conformity. Every nation that is now independent and wants to remain independent is involved in this grim, costly, distasteful division in the world, no matter how remote, no matter how uninterested. . . .

"If the United States and the other nations of the Western Hemisphere should accept this new phase of aggression we would be delinquent in our obligations to world peace. If the United States and the other nations of the Western Hemisphere should accept this basic disturbance of the world's structure of power we would invite a new surge of aggression at every point along the frontier. If we do not stand firm here our adversaries may think that we will stand firm nowhere—and we guarantee a heightening of the world civil war to new levels of intensity and peril. . . .

Let me ask you one simple question: Do you, Ambassador Zorin, deny that the USSR has placed and is placing medium and intermediate-range missiles and sites in Cuba? Yes or no? Do not wait for the interpretation. Yes or no?"

The President (translated from Russian): "I am not in an American court of law, and therefore do not wish to answer a question put to me in the manner of a prosecuting counsel. You will receive the answer in due course in my capacity as representative of the Soviet Union."

Mr. Stevenson: "You are in the courtroom of world opinion right now, and you can answer Yes or No. . . .

On Sunday morning, October 28, 1962, a message from Moscow reaches the White House: Khrushchev is withdrawing the missiles. The crisis passes as quickly as it arose, the world relaxes, congratulations pour in to Kennedy—it was a triumph of American firmness, restraint and good judgment. Nine months later the nuclear test ban is signed in Moscow, and Americans and Russians are exchanging toasts in Georgian champagne.

It was a famous victory. Yes, but seen from the Soviet side it was an intolerable humiliation. If it is proper for the

U.S. to install missiles in Turkey, which we have never attacked, they ask, why is it unacceptable for us to install missiles to defend Cuba which the U.S. only last year invaded at the Bay of Pigs? Never again will we permit ourselves to be so outclassed in armament that we shall have to submit so shamefully to American dictation. So the race in strategic and naval armaments redoubles in speed and scope. Ten years later the arsenals of the two superpowers are enormously magnified, approximately equal —and the two most powerful nations in history are more insecure than ever before.

Moscow: July 1971   Four Americans have been granted an interview by Alexei Kosygin, Prime Minister of the Soviet Union. They are General James Gavin, a leader of the Normandy invasion, Senator Frank Church of Idaho, David Rockefeller, chairman of the Chase Manhattan Bank, and the writer, a former Ambassador to the United Nations. They have just come from a private conference with Soviet colleagues in Kiev where disarmament, the environment, East–West trade and the United Nations were discussed with candor and goodwill.

Now they sit across a bare table from the Prime Minister in the Kremlin. Through the windows they see the golden onion-domes of the medieval churches and the cloudless azure sky. There is no sound of any kind save their voices.

Both sides agreed at Kiev, General Gavin reports, that less should be spent on armaments and more on other problems, such as protection of the environment. A sound idea, Kosygin agrees, but how to translate it into action? In order to settle political problems, says Church, we must build more confidence; but, having in mind modern means of surveillance, mutually beneficial arms-control agreements can be reached even without full confidence.

Kosygin pauses and reflects. This is the focal point in our relationship, he says, and on its solution will depend

the settlement of many other problems. Both sides want to
slow down the arms race; both have more than enough
strategic weapons. In any solution the status quo should
be preserved; neither side should be able to take advantage of the situation to make a leap forward. We are
conducting the SALT talks in all seriousness and want
results, but some confidence in the other *is* needed on both
sides. Arms could be hidden away in a "closed laboratory"
under pretense of abolition. We Soviets, he says, are in
favor of the total elimination of nuclear weapons, because
even limited or conventional war would be likely to develop into nuclear war.

Senator Church refers again to the mutual mistrust and
points out the difficulties which would be encountered in
the Senate even now for the ratification of a comprehensive test ban. Even partial agreements at SALT would be
useful. If we agree together, he says, we can keep the
peace of the world; if not, we have everything to lose.

But how can confidence be created and maintained?
Kosygin asks. During his visit to Glassboro he saw no
signs of mistrust on the part of the American people.
Sometimes he suspects it is artificially created. Have the
Soviets ever gone back on treaty commitments? No, of
course not. Those who want to prevent agreements use
mistrust as a smoke screen and manipulate it. If one side
likes to swim about in a neutral area, others will also be
tempted to respond in the same way and this will undermine confidence. We must move on a basis of equality
and thus overcome mistrust.

Senator Church pursues his point. One of the main
causes of mistrust is the great volume of armaments. If
these can be reduced, this would be the best help to
reestablishing mutual confidence. U.S. opinion, he assures
the Prime Minister, strongly favors success in the SALT
talks and improved U.S.–Soviet relations.

Yes, says Kosygin, he is deeply convinced that this is so.
Only an abnormal person could even think of conflict
between the two of us.

II

The Changing Environment of Foreign Affairs

Before examining how foreign affairs have been conducted and misconducted over recent decades, it will be useful to explain briefly, first, what the chief objects of diplomacy have traditionally been; and, second, what new conditions are displacing or eroding many of the old objects of this ancient game.

I use the word "game" advisedly. The stakes of foreign policy are deadly serious. Mistakes in its conduct have brought on two world wars in the past sixty years, caused enormous suffering and slaughter, and critically strained the fabric of Western civilization. Nothing is more real and can be more shattering than the consequences of mismanaged foreign affairs.

It is important to keep in mind, however, that foreign affairs are conducted not by rules but by men, by leaders and peoples conditioned by pride, fear, vanity and every other variety of human emotion, and that the rational objects put forward in explanation of policy are all too frequently rationalizations of these emotions.

The conduct of foreign affairs is too often reminiscent of small boys playing soldiers or king of the mountain, of juvenile gangs competing for territory and machismo. One sometimes wishes that the Great Earth Mother might one day appear, sweep up their toys and regalia, and send them all off to school or to bed.

The tragedy is that no one, or so it seems, can stop playing the game or change its objects until everyone else does. All of us, at least the big powers, have more or less to stop or to change together, and that is not easy to arrange.

Traditional Objects of Foreign Policy

The central traditional object of foreign policy has been that enigmatic and nebulous phenomenon: "national security." Even after two centuries of triumphant nationalism, it is still hard to define what a nation is, but once one of them has crystallized, whether it be a neat ethnic and geographic unit like Italy, a sprawling composite like the United States or the Soviet Union, or a haphazard creation of colonialism like so many Asian and African nations, it immediately becomes fanatically self-conscious and obsessed with the desire for self-preservation. Any national government considers, no doubt rightly as things stand, that its primary duty and interest is to deter external attack and to resist it successfully if it comes. That is the fundamental object of foreign policy.

Another significant object, at least of prudent national leaders, has been to avoid involvement in a major war. Traditionally, however, this object has been distinctly secondary, at least for the great powers, as appears from the fact that none of them has ever kept out of a major war for long and that all of them have been involved in two

great wars in this century. With the invention of nuclear
weapons, however, this object of foreign policy has begun
to be given almost equal weight as the first one, since it is
perceived that even a nuclear war that is "won" may be as
fatal to national security as one that is lost. The potential
incompatability between the first and second objects, between deterring nuclear attack and avoiding nuclear war,
has not yet been resolved and is at the heart of our gravest
dilemma.

The third object of foreign policy is all too often overlooked, because it is not usually avowed. The overriding
object of most governments is, of course, to stay in power.
They therefore must pursue a foreign policy which is at
least tolerable to the politically active part of the population, which may be a small elite in a totalitarian state or a
majority of the electorate in a democracy. The often-
decisive effect of domestic opinion on the conduct of
foreign policy, the need for governments to develop and
maintain a fair measure of domestic consensus is under-
estimated by both policy-makers and historians. Also, it is
extremely rare that governments objectively weigh the
needs of "national security" against those of domestic
welfare, unless outraged electorates oblige them to do so.

Another significant and sometimes decisive object of
foreign policy is the promotion of national power, influence and prestige abroad. This object has many facets.
It may merely be the laudable cultivation of as many
friends as possible. It may involve the creation of defensive alliances, the establishment of overseas bases, or the
waging of limited wars to prevent strategic points from
falling to an adversary. It may go so far as to involve the
propagation of a faith, a religion or an ideology, whether
by missionary endeavor, by subversion, by insurgency or
by overt military attack across frontiers. There may also be
military aggression with purely national rather than ideological content. Sometimes the predominant motive is

only the vainglory of a national leader, and the main object of his foreign policy the gratification of that vanity.

A further object of foreign policy, which has changed its emphasis in recent times, is the pursuit of economic gain by the nation or its elite. In the old days this expressed itself in looting and pillage or in the seizure and exploitation of colonies. Happily, it is now more often a cultivation of bilateral and multilateral benefits arising from trade, overseas investment and economic development. This is an object zealously sought by all nations, but arousing passionate resentment on the part of economically weaker countries when it results—as it almost always does—in partial dependence on foreigners and some infringement of absolute national sovereignty.

Finally—and this is a very new and rudimentary object of foreign policy, condescendingly viewed by most chiefs of government and foreign offices—there is the fostering of multilateral cooperation among nations and the strengthening of international institutions designed to implement this cooperation. I shall have more to say later about this object of policy, which in a rational world would have the highest priority.

New Conditions to Which Foreign Policy Must Adapt

All human institutions and practices must adapt to changing conditions or perish. At most times in history, conditions have changed almost imperceptibly and there has been ample time to adapt. Even so, civilizations have more often than not failed to do so; Toynbee lists more than a dozen that have disappeared, some into almost total oblivion.

At other times historical change proceeds with breathtaking speed and only the most agile and adroit adapt and survive. Today, thanks to science and technology, change has become vertiginous, and, since it is likely to accelerate even more, there is serious question whether any society can hold together. As Paul Valéry said more than fifty years ago, "We see now that the abyss of history is large enough for everyone. We sense now that a civilization is just as fragile as a life."*

Another odd fact is that this process of change has been wildly discrepant in different parts of the world, even inside individual nations and especially inside men's heads, so that there is in fact no single consistent twentieth-century pattern, but only a welter of clashing patterns, most of them obsolete. As Thomas Hughes has recently written: "Half-seriously, one can say that the twentieth century is currently made up of fourteenth-century farmers, fifteenth-century theologians, sixteenth-century politicians, seventeenth-century economists, eighteenth-century bureaucrats, nineteenth-century generals and twenty-first-century scientists."† I would disagree only with the last of these judgments; most living scientists seem to me still about a quarter century behind our times and its imperatives.

All this is commonplace, and is mentioned here only because of the need to emphasize that present-day makers of foreign affairs are confronted with problems of wholly unprecedented dimensions, that many of the traditional objects of foreign policy make little or no sense under the new conditions, and that therefore there is likely to be, even on the part of the most skilled operators, more misconduct than wise conduct of foreign affairs. Even policy correctly designed to cope with a problem ten years ago may be wholly out of phase with what has happened

*Paul Valéry, *Oeuvres I 988* (1919), quoted by George Ball in *Discipline of Power* (Boston: Little Brown, 1968).
†*Foreign Affairs*, April 1972.

in the meantime—and even more with what will happen in the next ten years.

These new conditions are no secret. They have been enormously publicized, exhaustively explained and persistently disregarded.

First is the proliferation of nuclear weapons. If a full-scale nuclear war should break out between the United States and the Soviet Union, it is conservatively estimated that about a hundred million people in each country, nearly half the population of each, would die within the first few days. Others would die during succeeding weeks and months from the effects of radiation and fallout, and from the disease, starvation and violence resulting from the breakdown of government, industry, transportation and public services. What would remain, for a period of unpredictable duration, would be a state of anarchy and devastation such as has not existed since the early Middle Ages.

Of course, this state would not be limited to the two nations mentioned; it would also presumably include at least their allies in Western and Eastern Europe. The effect on the rest of the world of fallout and of the elimination of Europe and North America from the world economy might be disastrous. No less an authority than Dean Rusk has said that "World War III would mean the end of organized government in the Northern Hemisphere." Yet as long as the weapons are there, deployed and ready to use at a moment's notice, this could happen, no matter what elaborate precautions are taken, no matter how strong the determination of governments to prevent it. This is a situation which has never before existed in history.

Another such situation is the population explosion. All of the millennia from the first appearance of man until about 1830 were required to produce the first billion human beings. It took another century, until 1930, to produce the second billion, and only thirty years, until

1960, to produce the third. We shall very probably reach the fourth billion within fifteen years, by 1975. United Nations experts predict that by the year 2000, world population will be between six and a half and seven billion, of which over a billion would be Chinese and another billion Indian. Obviously, if the majority of mankind continues to reproduce at present rates, we would reach ten billion early in the twenty-first century and twenty billion a very few decades later.

The population explosion is already preventing the substantial economic growth which has occurred in many poor countries from having much effect on per-capita income and individual standards of living. The best that can be said in many places is that many more people are living no worse than many fewer were living a short time ago. But if all of them—all 3.6 billion now on the planet—enjoyed the same standard of living the 210 million Americans do, the accumulation of wastes and pollution of the environment might well be more than the biosphere could stand. Yet if the gap between rich and poor nations continues to widen, as seems likely if population growth is unchecked, the chances for international stability will be extremely meager.

Moreover, studies of overcrowding among animals reveal patterns first of epidemic violence and then of chronic apathy, sexual abnormality and cannibalism. Up to a point, men can protect themselves from the exigencies of nature, but they are not indefinitely exempt from its laws. The population explosion, like nuclear weaponry, will, if allowed to proceed without effective inhibition, so revolutionize the conditions under which governments must conduct their foreign relations that the traditional rules and objects established during the five millennia of human civilization could very suddenly become irrelevant.

The other new conditions which are eroding the objects which foreign policy has traditionally pursued may be mentioned more briefly. Transport and communication have become so swift that leaving political obstacles aside, a man could meet face to face almost any other man in the world within a matter of hours, and could speak to him, if not with him, almost instantaneously. This makes the world smaller in many respects than Rhode Island was in 1776.

Despite the shrinking of the globe there are about sixty more independent sovereign nations on it than there were thirty years ago. The world is being integrated physically and Balkanized politically. There are now no less than a hundred and thirty separate "national securities" and national foreign policies to be reconciled with each other.

At the same time, *economically* the developed nations are being increasingly integrated, avowedly in the Common Market and the Group of Ten, surreptitiously through the multinational corporation. Yet this creeping integration, progressive and profitable as it seems, has its liabilities as well as its assets. The interdependence which has already taken place makes all nations vulnerable to measures adopted by one for purely domestic reasons. When, without prior consultation, the United States detaches the dollar from gold and imposes an import surcharge, the livelihood of Japanese, Germans and Argentines is jeopardized. Economic interdependence has grown far more rapidly than the international machinery necessary to rationalize and manage it.

Meanwhile, the less developed nations, which for centuries existed in a state of suspended political animation, are endeavoring to telescope into decades the evolution which Europeans experienced over a thousand years and have not yet completed. Economically the new nations are agonizingly ambivalent, desiring and often expecting to catch up quickly with the rich and needing their help to do so, yet fearful that the vast disparity of power between them will enable the rich to use aid and investment to reimpose the colonialism from which the poor have only just escaped.

Both may be confronting an even more tragic dilemma.

World production of goods essential to modern society can only grow to a certain point, still undetermined but already vaguely apprehended, without imposing intolerable stresses on an environment necessary for human survival. We may not be too far distant from that ceiling. Each new human life, each new effective demand for what modern society promises, brings production closer to the ceiling. When it is reached, poverty can no longer be alleviated by further production growth, but only by redistribution of what is being produced under the tolerable ceiling. The consequences for international relations of an imperative demand for such redistribution between rich and poor nations can be imagined. Under these unprecedented circumstances any increase in population would inescapably mean a lower per-capita income, first in the country where the increase occurred, but eventually everywhere.

Finally, a cultural and educational explosion is taking place. While illiteracy is still very substantial, a larger proportion of the world's population learns each year to read. Remote and backward villages have their ears glued to transistor radios; TV aerials sprout riotously over more and more of the world's cities. In 1910 only about 13 percent of the people twenty-five years old and over in the United States had finished high school and 2.7 percent had finished college; in 1970 the corresponding figures were 55 percent for high school graduates and 11 percent for college graduates. A majority of other countries are moving with increasing speed in the same direction. This educational explosion is creating almost overnight both a new constituency and a new condition with which makers of foreign policy must cope if they are to stay in power.

Nevertheless, it is equally clear that the educational revolution has hardly begun to meet the needs of the times. Indeed, one of the most acute students of our technological society, Aurelio Peccei* holds that despite

The Chasm Ahead (New York: Macmillan, 1969).

its vast proliferation, education today is more discrepant with the requirements of life in contemporary society than was the education, no matter how elementary, of any previous age. The gap between what young men and women learn and what they need to know is wider than it ever was—so far has technology outstripped knowledge.

Education can and should be the beginning of wisdom. It can also be, and often is, the beginning of frustrated expectations, of disillusion and disorientation, of Utopian dreams and violent revolution. Almost everything that was accepted as gospel a hundred years ago, and much that was accepted as gospel twenty years ago, is fundamentally questioned, if not contemptuously rejected. This can be good if it represents an intelligent adaptation to the new conditions just described; it can be fatal if it becomes merely a blind flight to new gospels no more pertinent and rational than the old ones.

III
The
Conduct and Misconduct
of Foreign Affairs

The relevance of history has always been, and is now more than ever, disputed. Sometimes the same person is of two minds about it.

In his *Souvenirs* De Tocqueville wrote: "The history of our times, however new and unexpected it may seem, always belongs at the bottom to the old history of humanity, and what we call new facts are often nothing more than facts forgotten." In the same book, however, he also wrote: "I have always observed that in politics people were often ruined through possessing too good a memory . . . So true is it that, if humanity be always the same, the course of history is always different, that the past is not able to teach us much concerning the present . . ."

In the latter judgment he may have had in mind what concerned the historian J. H. Plumb* when he wrote recently: "The past is always a created ideology with a

* *The Death of the Past* (Boston: Houghton Mifflin, 1970).

purpose, designed to control individuals, to motivate societies, or inspire classes. Nothing has been so corruptly used as concepts of the past. The future of history and historians is to cleanse the story of mankind from those deceiving visions of a purposeful past."

One can perhaps impartially conclude that history is relevant, often decisively so; that one cannot, however, simplistically predict the present or the future from the past because the most relevant factors are often those most easily overlooked or most blindly disregarded; that the unexamined past is usually misleading and often, as Plumb says, corrupting, because it transmits deeply imprinted error and rationalization; and that indeed history is only relevant and useful if it is scrutinized with the utmost rigor.

The purpose of this section of the book is to scrutinize the claims, the intentions and the behavior of some of those who have been responsible for the conduct of foreign policy in the largest nations during the past forty years. This scrutiny will be based on an attempt to show how the professed object of foreign policy—the pursuit of the national interest—has been distorted or wholly lost, and how policy itself has been warped by political, ideological, professional and personal factors anchored in the past and often irrelevant to the realities of the present.

Disorientation Caused by Domestic Factors

Leaders and policy-makers are, far more often than they like to admit, prisoners of their own domestic opinion—of the convictions of electorates or elites which may constrain the leaders either to undertake what they know to be folly or to fail to do what they know to be necessary. Of course, the leaders often share the delusions of their people. Sometimes they were responsible for instilling or magnifying the delusions in the first place and have subsequently come to recognize their mistakes, but find themselves swept along by the very passions they helped unleash.

The history of the twentieth century is replete with examples of this phenomenon. There was no really logical reason why at the beginning of the century the great powers of Europe should have been lined up in just the way they were: Germany, Austria and Italy versus England, France and Russia. England and France had been at war with Russia in the 1850's, and Germany and Italy at war with Austria in the 1860's. England had almost allied itself with Germany rather than France at the opening of the new century. Yet in the decade before 1914 the peoples of these two alliances each became so persuaded of the malevolence and aggressive intentions of the other that each entered World War I with almost juvenile enthusiasm, certain of the total righteousness of its cause.

As the consequent enormous bloodletting continued year after year the leaders felt called upon to exaggerate—in order to maintain the war effort and the willingness to die—both the responsibility and the iniquity of the enemy and the purity and rationality of their own objectives. So well did they perform this task that at the end of the war public and parliamentary opinion among the victors demanded a punitive peace, which was not only unjustified by the origins of the war but which fatally undermined the German republic and paved the way for Hitler. There was a vicious circle of international disaster in which irrational mutual hostility was so intensely generated that it could not be abated, even by leaders who saw it should be, in time to make the peace of reconciliation which might have prevented another war.

But this was not the end. During the twenties the peoples of Europe woke up to the fact that they had been grossly deceived about the origins and objects of the war, the glorious future that awaited them after victory, and the inborn villainy of their fellow Europeans across frontiers. Everyone read Remarque's *All Quiet on the Western Front* and the revisionist histories of G. Lowes Dickinson, Fabre Luce and Sidney Fay. The Oxford Union voted not "to fight for King and country." At this point the Nazis seized power in Germany. The peoples of France and England, however, believing they had learned their lesson, opted for appeasement and refused to permit measures of defense necessary under the new circumstances to prevent still another war. They tolerated the militarization of the Rhineland, the seizure of Austria and the dismemberment of Czechoslovakia. Only when Hitler was uncontrollably intoxicated by success did they reluctantly and still half-heartedly decide to stand up to him.

Popular opinion in America, being both less sophisticated and less involved, vacillated even more sharply and imposed equally foolish constraints on its leaders. Having been swept into World War I by the extravagant exhortations of the Anglophiles and Francophiles, by the prospect of a "war to end wars" and a "world made safe for democracy," they reacted quickly and decisively against the rapacity of the victors and the chaos of postwar Europe by dropping out into obstinate isolationism, from which only Pearl Harbor recalled them.

It is therefore proper to say of the conduct of foreign affairs by the democracies between the two wars that it was so inhibitied first by the inflammation and then by the disillusionment of public opinion that even wise leaders —and there were not many of them—had little impact or freedom of maneuver. Peace was made too late with the German republic; containment was conceived too late to check the Third Reich.

Somewhat analogous currents played a significant part during the Cold War and its aftermath. Western opinion had been for the most part hostile to the Soviet regime between the two wars; this hostility had been aggravated by Stalin's purges of the late thirties and the Stalin–Hitler pact of 1939. Nevertheless, the spirit of comradeship and common purpose generated by the shared struggle against the Nazis created in the West, at least, a tentative predisposition toward continued cooperation, a predisposition which was reflected in the United Nations Charter but which was probably in fact never more than skin-deep.

It was remarkable how quickly and easily it was shattered. When Molotov came through Washington on his way to the San Francisco Conference in April 1945, the new President, taking somewhat too literally the advice his experts gave him, lectured the Soviet Foreign Minister like a schoolboy. "I have never been talked to like that in my life," Truman quotes him as replying. A few months later a speech by Stalin—reflecting, as one reads it today, merely standard Marxist rhetoric—was widely interpreted in the West, as James Forrestal confided to his diary at the time, as a declaration of war on the world. Churchill responded almost at once with even more gaudy rhetoric in his "Iron Curtain" speech at Fulton, Missouri. There was already an enormous reservoir of ill will and mistrust between East and West, camouflaged during the war but boiling up to the surface of public awareness the moment the war ended. It is doubtful that even Roosevelt, had he lived, could have contained it.

In fact, little or no effort was made on either side to do so. Stalin's foreign policy in the five years after the war—the seizure of most of Eastern Europe, the Greek civil war, the Berlin blockade, the coup d'état in Prague, the attack on South Korea—amply confirmed the Western leaders' convictions about Communism and created anxieties about Communist designs probably far outrunning the real intentions of Stalin and Mao. Little was needed to stir up public opinion in the West to passionate anti-Communism, which indeed soon outstripped and even turned against some of the leaders who first invoked it. Within five years of victory Joseph McCarthy was in the saddle in America, and around the world the Cold War was in full swing.

An instructive example of the interaction between official policy and domestic factors is reflected in Joseph Jones's account* of the formulation of the Truman Doctrine. The reason for urgent U.S. action in February 1947 was the need for massive military and economic aid to Greece in the Communist-provoked civil war and the inability of Britain any longer to meet that need. A related but less critical requirement was for similar but smaller aid to Turkey.

The original intention of those confronted with the problem in the State Department was to confine the presentation to Congress to those two countries. However, when, in a preliminary meeting with Congressional leaders in the White House on February 27, Secretary George C. Marshall set forth the case in these relatively modest terms, he awoke no enthusiasm; rather, there was some conventional grumbling that we were preparing "to pull the British chestnuts out of the fire." Undersecretary Acheson thereupon stepped into the breach and expounded in sweeping and dramatic terms the threat to the whole "free world" posed by Soviet expansion over the preceding eighteen months. This exposition deeply impressed and for the most part persuaded the audience. Indeed, Senator Arthur Vandenberg, president pro tempore of the Senate and chairman of the Foreign Relations Committee in the new Republican Congress, made clear his view that any request to the Congress for Greek–Turkish aid must be presented, if it were to win the approval of the Congress and the American people, in the same broad context which Acheson had so grimly and convincingly described.

Consequently the President's message to Congress of March 12, the famous Truman Doctrine, was

---

The Fifteen Weeks (New York: Viking Press, 1955).

phrased—much to the dismay, for example, of George Kennan who had participated in the preliminary planning—not in terms of a limited program to succor two countries, but as a global commitment "to support free peoples who are resisting attempted subjugation by armed minorities or by outside pressure." This phrasing was consciously formulated with a view to having the most telling impact on Congress and the public and hence of assuring prompt approval by the former of Greek–Turkish aid. Thus, because it was assumed that public support of limited and necessary objectives could only be assured by stating them in apocalyptic terms, as part of a world-wide struggle between good and evil, a doctrine was put forward, a precedent was set, and a moral commitment was assumed which was far more comprehensive and open-ended than the circumstances required; which helped create an enduring and militant climate of opinion in the United States; and which, two decades later, was to lure three other American Presidents into the morass of Vietnam.

Already in the late 1940's and early 1950's a similar reciprocal escalation of passion and commitment between leaders and public had occurred in regard to China. Here the initial fault may have lain with Roosevelt, who, for quite respectable reasons, elevated Nationalist China to membership in the Big Five and helped build up a deceptive image of the virtues, capacities and staying power of its government vis-à-vis the Communists. The inflammation of public opinion in this case, however, was carried out by professional friends of the Nationalists, organized into the "China lobby," and by the Republican Party, excluded from power for two decades and desperate for an issue on which to climb back.

When the Nationalist collapse occurred, their patrons and friends blamed not the incompetence and corruption of the Chiang Kai-shek regime but the Democratic administration. When the latter published a white paper demonstrating where the responsibility for failure lay, the Republicans rallied behind McCarthy to claim that China was "lost" not by the Nationalist Chinese but by the China experts in the Foreign Service who had predicted this outcome. I worked on the China white paper myself and luckily escaped with my skin, but others less lucky were hounded out of the service. So profound and enduring a false image of realities in China was imprinted on the public mind that twenty-two years were to pass before an American administration, a Republican one at that, finally felt it politically safe to admit what everyone had known all that time—that Mao, not Chiang, ruled China and was entitled to represent it in the United Nations. A more impressive and depressing example of the folly of inspiring false myths in the public mind can hardly be imagined.

I might also cite from personal experience an example of another side of the coin—a case in which leaders failed to seize an opportunity to abate the Cold War because they feared public opinion would thereby be unduly mellowed and relaxed.

In early 1958 my assignment as ambassador to Syria was abruptly terminated by the union of that country with Egypt, and I was called back to Washington until a new post could be found for me. One of the temporary jobs given me there was to help in contingency planning for the East–West summit meeting for which Khrushchev had been assiduously pressing. It soon became obvious that the last thing the President and Secretary of State as well as other Western leaders desired was a summit meeting with the Soviets, and that they would only be dragged to one at the last possible moment and after having publicly made it as clear as they could that nothing would or could be accomplished. Considering the great importance of the issues outstanding between East and West, this may seem a curious attitude, but it arose not so much from the Western leaders' mistrust of the Soviets as from their mistrust of their own people.

At bottom they were convinced that the basic issues between them and the Russians were non-negotiable, that Khrushchev's intention to "bury" the West was genuine and ineradicable, and that the keystone of successful resistance to the Soviets must be the inflexible maintenance of a strong and united Western military posture. They were acutely aware, however, that the prolonged maintenance of such a posture was both psychologically and fiscally unpopular with large segments of the Western electorate. They were afraid that the voting public would seize any excuse to cut military budgets and reduce NATO obligations, and that the spectacle on television of Eisenhower and Khrushchev in smiling embrace, the impact of the ritually harmonious communiqués which must be issued even in the absence of substantive agreements, would provide just such an excuse. So they dragged their feet and delayed the summit meeting for about two years, until May 1960.

While, of course, one cannot be certain, the tragedy was that apparently in 1958 and 1959 Khrushchev may—for internal reasons—have been genuinely seeking limited accommodations with the West on some issues and may have staked his prestige inside the Soviet hierarchy on achieving them. He was a vain and sensitive man who derived great emotional satisfaction from being received as an equal by prestigious Western leaders. His visit to the United States in 1959 made a deep and favorable impression upon him and might conceivably have marked a turning point in East–West relations had it been followed swiftly either by a return visit by Eisenhower to the Soviet Union or by the long-delayed summit.

Instead, however, both the summit and the visit were held off for another eight months, and in the meantime Western leaders took pains to announce in unmistakable terms, for the benefit of their own public, that they would concede nothing in forthcoming negotiations and that nothing would be accomplished. It is quite conceivable that the failure of Khrushchev's two-year campaign to negotiate so weakened his position with his colleagues in the Kremlin that, when the summit did at last convene in Paris in May 1960, he felt obliged to use the U-2 episode as a pretext to abort it. Far worse, rebuffed and furious, he turned for the next two and a half years from a policy of negotiation to one of confrontation. The Berlin crisis of 1961 and the missile crisis of 1962 were a partial result.

There are many depressing examples of international conflicts in which leaders have first aroused their own people against a neighbor and then discovered to their chagrin that even when they judged the time had come to move toward peace, they were prisoners of the popular passions they had stimulated. The slightest suggestion of compromise was at once stigmatized as betrayal, and the conflicts persisted and escalated long after a realistic balance sheet for either side showed liabilities far outweighing assets.

This was true of the Arabs, who several times rejected opportunities to make a reasonable peace with Israel because they had so often rhetorically committed themselves to its destruction. It became equally true of the Israelis, who, when Egypt in 1971 at long last agreed to make peace, responded with demands for territorial expansion, which their leaders had told them was vital to "security," but which in fact precluded the peace agreement they had so long sought.

Perhaps an even more odd phenomenon is the impact of American opinion on the Vietnam war. In this case I would suggest that in the first three years of major U.S. involvement, public opinion did not in fact exercise either a stimulating or an inhibiting effect on the leadership, but that the leaders' *recollection* of the domestic political consequences of the "loss" of China, and their fear of similar consequences to them if Vietnam were "lost," was perhaps the decisive factor in determining their policy and behavior. Even after public opposition to the war had begun to manifest itself so dramatically as to induce President Johnson not to run for reelection, President Nixon continued to be so convinced that the "silent majority" would still react with political fury to a defeat in Vietnam that for four more years he pursued the will-o-the-wisp of winning the war while withdrawing from it. Indeed, by the rhetoric he used in explaining the slow pace of his withdrawal—for example, his description of the U.S. as a "pitiful helpless giant" if it failed to react to provocation—he contributed to the very syndromes in the public mind which he professed to fear. So even if these two Presidents misread domestic opinion, they responded compulsively to what they *thought* it to be. In so doing, one destroyed himself politically and the other prolonged and aggravated the tragic divisions inside his own country.

In fact, a plausible case can be made that the two controlling architects of U.S. foreign policy during the entire period from 1945 to the present day have been Joseph Stalin and Joseph McCarthy: the first, because he aroused in American leaders and people extravagant fears of mortal threat to their national security; the second, because he created in the minds of American Presidents even more poignant and personal fears that if they were held responsible for any "loss" of territory or position anywhere to Communism, they would be swept aside by an outraged electorate. The paradox was that too often their own miscalculated rhetoric paralleled and confirmed that of McCarthy.

Another form of disorientation of foreign policy arising from domestic factors might be mentioned in conclusion: the effect on policy of a powerful pressure group or lobby, acting in most cases in what it claims to be the national interest but in fact inspired and stimulated by the interest of a particular foreign government with which the pressure group has emotional or economic ties. Outstanding examples of this phenomenon would be, in the United States, the so-called China lobby, already mentioned; the related group which staunchly supported Diem in Vietnam and enabled him to defy for so long official U.S. pressure for political and economic reform; and most successful of all, the highly organized and well-endowed pro-Israel lobby, activated and directed whenever the need arises by the Israeli embassy in Washington, which is able almost overnight to mobilize Congressional majorities for any bill or appropriation favorable to Israel.

There is another, more conventional kind of lobby—that representing particular business interests but sometimes exercising, for complicated political reasons, leverage over the foreign policy of an administration all out of proportion to the real significance of those interests to the national economy. There have been at least two recent examples. U.S.–Japanese relations, of critical importance to our whole Asian strategy and already strained by the sudden shifts in our China and financial policies in the summer of 1971, were further seriously compromised in the autumn by our forcing on the Japanese a textile "agreement" limiting their exports to us. The proportion of the U.S. textile market actually held by the Japanese was extremely small, but the President had made a political commitment to the textile industry, and apparently he felt it of overriding importance to his "Southern strategy" that he carry it out before the next election.

In a similar way, at the end of 1971 a chrome lobby was able to induce the Congress, with only perfunctory administration opposition, to repeal the ban on chrome imports from Rhodesia, despite the fact that doing so involved a breach of our treaty commitments to the United Nations, further fractured UN sanctions against Rhodesia, and gratuitously concentrated against the United States the frustration and anger of the Black African nations.

There is an ever-present danger of other protectionist lobbies prevailing in the same way, in blissful disregard of the part which, for example, the Smoot-Hawley tariff of 1930 played in deepening the depression in Europe, helping bring Hitler to power and thus provoking World War II.

As in most aspects of the highly inexact science of foreign affairs, no clear-cut conclusion can be drawn from these examples of the effect of domestic opinion and pressure on foreign policy. Tentatively one might say that the man in the street normally has no strong interest in foreign affairs; that he has, however, prejudices about foreigners which are easily aroused and less easily quieted; and that when his emotions about foreign issues are at last thoroughly excited they are likely to persist long after they have ceased to be relevant—although in fact they sometimes do not persist as long as leaders, particularly those sharing the emotions, anticipate they will.

As to the leaders, their paramount concern, whether or not they admit it even to themselves, is almost always to stay in power. They are profoundly and sincerely convinced that, whatever compromises and mistakes they may make, their opponents would make worse ones, and that it is in their country's interest—indeed their own patriotic duty—to remain in office.

Therefore, while they may manipulate or hoodwink their own public (in the public's interest, of course), they will take care, if they possibly can, not to become so separated from it as to be thrown out. Hence the conduct of foreign affairs, only slightly less than the conduct of domestic affairs, is geared to wayward or irrational currents of public opinion, is circumscribed by what the leaders think the public will tolerate at any given moment, and is able only rarely and surreptitiously to look beyond the next election.

Thus, all too often, leaders and led reciprocally debase each other, and while the one is hungry for confidence and the latter for direction, each shows the other his pettiest side. Foreign policy comes to reflect not high ideals or even real interests, but the most primitive emotions and the meanest private pretensions.

Disorientation Arising from Ideologies and Causes

A related characteristic of an age when larger segments of the population, or at least larger elites, participate in public affairs is the enormously disorienting effect of popular ideologies and causes on international relations.

This phenomenon is far from new. Relations between the peoples of Europe and of the Near East were determined for about five centuries by the struggle between Christianity and Islam, manifesting itself first in the prodigious Western thrust of the Crusades and then in the equally intense Eastern counterthrust of the Ottoman Empire. Inside Europe, fanatical hostility between Christian sects governed and corrupted relations between states for a hundred years in the sixteenth and seventeenth centuries and led to barbarous ideological wars. An ideology fusing both nationalism and the rights of man inspired the French armies that swept across Europe at the end of the eighteenth century, and many popular revolts that subsequently triumphed or failed elsewhere.

Some of these same ideological elements animated many of the participants in World War I. Self-determination of peoples was the heart of Wilson's Fourteen Points, and "making the world safe for democracy" was one of the professed war aims of the Entente Powers. The consequence was the breakup of the Austrian, German and Russian empires, the further Balkanization of Eastern Europe, and its vulnerability first to Hitler and then to Stalin. In the subsequent half century the disintegration of empires and the triumph of nationalism have become world-wide.

Most recently, the principle of self-determination was embodied in the United Nations Charter in 1945, and since that time has become the First Commandment of the Third World. Independence and UN membership are now the accepted symbols of collective dignity. More than sixty new nations have been so consecrated since 1945, and many others, including a bevy of "ministates," are still clamoring to be born. Even inside the older countries, Flemings, Welsh, Basques, Bretons, Croats, Kurds and French-Canadians struggle for national identity borrowed from a distant past and quite disregardful of a rational future. Many of the new nations, mosaics of linguistic and tribal units artificially assembled by European colonizers, hang together by the skin of their teeth. The process of "self-determination," unsuccessful in Biafra but successful in Bangladesh, continues to whittle more states to smaller and less viable dimensions.

The idea of nationhood—as a cultural entity more compelling than religion, as a governmental entity more cohesive and efficient than either feudalism or empire—has had an enormous and deserved success in modern times. It has drawn and constantly redrawn the map of the world. It still holds the passionate loyalty of more human beings than any other collective idea. It is at the height of its power and the beginning of its decline. It is the most stupendous of political anachronisms, the most contemporary and the most archaic of systems of government.

The most conspicuous new religion of the twentieth century is that expounded and revised by Marx, Lenin and Mao. This is not the place to analyze or pass judgment on socialism, but the pertinence to the conduct of foreign affairs of Marxism as an evangelistic ideology and of Communism as a crusading political system is incontestable. The weakness of the Soviet Union before World War

II prevented its playing a leading role in world politics, though even during that quarter century its doctrine was the nightmare of Western statesmen, the mirage of many Western intellectuals and the pretext for Fascist dictators. After the war, however, the whole course of international relations was conditioned by the expansion of the Soviet Union over Eastern and Central Europe and its emergence as a military superpower; the capture by Communism of China, half of Vietnam and half of Korea; the acute fear of Western leaders that the Communists would be satisfied with nothing less than world domination; and the global competition and confrontation between East and West which resulted.

It is therefore plausible to characterize the mid-twentieth century as another age of religious or ideological wars, even though the hydrogen bomb kept the wars limited and although, as in most religious wars, national ambitions and rivalries were inextricably lodged in the ideological matrix. One might say that Communist states, such as the Soviet Union and North Vietnam, fought defensive wars when they had to, as nations, but offensive wars when they could, as crusaders.

The magnificent defense of the Soviet Union against the Nazi invasion was rightly called the Great Patriotic War. The pursuit of the Germans to Berlin and beyond, however, while justified by the urge to destroy Hitler and impose unconditional surrender, offered Stalin an apparently irresistible opportunity both to set up a wide defensive barrier against future attacks on Russia and to impose Communist regimes on the Eastern European nations. The penalty for his yielding to that temptation was to generate against the Soviet Union a host of enemies who, had she been less greedy, would have been only too glad to remain passively, if not actively, friendly.

The Communists had long been deluded into the conviction that theirs was a doctrine as "scientific"—that is, as exact and predictable—as the laws of physics, that they

were an elite naturally selected and metaphysically ordained to propagate the doctrine and carry its benefits to
all mankind, and that those who resisted them were by
definition unenlightened, degenerate and destined to early
extinction. This sense of being scientifically and inevitably allied with the future was immensely exhilarating
and profoundly corrupting; it was also as alien to exact
science as most social speculation is, and it was as certain
as any other display of self-righteousness to provoke an
equally extravagant response from those subjected to it.

Moreover, Americans have inherited from their Puritan
forebears a tendency to be self-righteous and evangelistic.
While they do not pretend that their social creeds—liberty,
democracy and free enterprise—are as "scientific" as the
Marxists do, this prudence does little to diminish their
conviction that these doctrines are incomparably the best
available and that all other men everywhere would be
better off under their benevolent aegis. Fortunately Americans have rarely tried, for long at least, to impose their
creeds by force, but when during these critical years and
thereafter they saw the Communists seeking over wide
areas of the globe to *suppress* them by force, our reaction
was quick and passionate. Five years of fighting one brand
of expansive totalitarianism and five years of confronting
another were sufficient to move the United States from
isolationism into an anti-Communist crusade of cosmic
proportions. Little heed was paid, in this connection or in
many others, to the sort of warning George Kennan had
inserted in a report to the State Department from Moscow
early in 1946: "After all, the greatest danger that can befall
us in coping with this problem of Soviet Communism is
that we shall allow ourselves to become like those with
whom we are coping."*

The American conversion was epitomized by a series of

---

*George Kennan, *Memoirs 1925–1950* (Boston: Little, Brown, 1967), p.
559.

stirring pronouncements over a number of years by many distinguished statesmen. A few brief excerpts will suggest their flavor and help to explain how crusades, even those arising in defensive response to other crusades, tend to be propelled by their own momentum onto uncharted, reef-strewn seas.

The first quotation is from President Truman's message to Congress on March 12, 1947—the Truman Doctrine. Its origin in the need for aid to Greece and Turkey and its extravagant enlargement in order to gain Congressional and public support have been described earlier. Excerpts from the Doctrine are quoted here in the context of the countercrusade against Communism which it came to inspire, to serve and to magnify.

> At the present moment in world history nearly every nation must choose between alternative ways of life. The choice is too often not a free one.
> One way of life is based upon the will of the majority, and is distinguished by free institutions, representative government, free elections, guarantees of individual liberty, freedom of speech and religion, and freedom from political oppression.
> The second way of life is based upon the will of the minority forcibly imposed upon the majority. It relies upon terror and oppression, controlled press and radio, fixed elections, and the suppression of personal freedoms.
> I believe that it must be the policy of the United States to support free peoples who are resisting attempted subjugation by armed minorities or by outside pressures.

(It might be noted that the moral impact of Truman's sweeping promise of support to peoples professing "a way of life . . . based upon the will of the majority and . . . distinguished by free institutions, representative government, free elections . . ." was in course of time somewhat diminished by its extension to gentlemen as little wedded to these principles as Franco, Salazar, Papadopoulos, Yahya Khan, Diem and Thieu. These leaders may in some cases have deserved aid on other grounds, but they were no more appropriate beneficiaries of a crusade than were the Teutonic Knights. Indeed, U.S. sanctimoniousness was sometimes skating on thin ice even when it confined its claims of a democratic way of life to itself. Averell Harriman quotes Khrushchev as asking him in 1959: "Do you expect to convince me that the voters of New York State had 'free elections' when their only choice for Governor was between a Rockefeller and a Harriman?"*)

The second quotation in these glimpses of American evangelism is from a statement made in Paris by Secretary of State Dean Acheson three years later, on May 8, 1950: "The United States Government, convinced that neither national independence nor democratic evolution exists in any area dominated by Soviet imperialism, considers the situation to be such as to warrant its according economic aid and military equipment to the Associated States of Indochina and France in order to assist them in restoring stability . . ."†

This statement is notable for three points: first, it applied the Truman Doctrine to Indochina, where the French were resisting another insurgency in which Communism and Vietnamese nationalism were inextricably mingled; second, it assumed that this insurgency, even in a region so distant from Moscow, was an instrument of "Soviet imperialism"; and third, despite Truman's reservation that "our help should be primarily through economic and financial aid," already at this early date our help "to the Associated States of Indochina and to France" included "military equipment," as, of course, it already had in large amounts to Greece and Turkey.

The third quotation is from a prominent spokesman of the Eisenhower Administration, Assistant Secretary of State Walter Robertson, in a speech delivered to the

*Chester Cooper, *The Lost Crusade* (New York: Dodd, Mead, 1970), p. 443.
†*Department of State Bulletin,* May 22, 1950.

American Legion in August 1954 shortly after the close of the conference which divided Vietnam and produced the Geneva Accords. Mr. Robertson said, "What is of the first importance now is to prevent further Communist expansion—first, by arousing Asia's unwitting masses to an awareness of the ruthless enslavement which threatens them; and second, by the rapid organization of a collective defense pact in Southeast Asia."*

It is difficult to decide whether what was most notable in this statement was the sanguine belief that American exhortation and example could arouse "Asia's unwitting masses" to our sort of awareness, or whether it was the rapid development of the Truman Doctrine from "primarily economic and financial aid" through "military equipment" to "a collective defense pact." The underlying and hazardous assumption behind the latter conception was that an instrument such as NATO, which had proved so effective in Europe, could be successfully transplanted, as SEATO, into the very different soil of East Asia.

The fourth and last quotation is from President Kennedy's Inaugural Address:

> Let every nation know, whether it wishes us well or ill, that we shall pay any price, bear any burden, meet any hardship, support any friend, oppose any foe to assure the survival and the success of liberty.
> This much we pledge—and more . . .
> In the long history of the world, only a few generations have been granted the role of defending freedom in its hour of maximum danger. I do not shrink from this responsibility—I welcome it. I do not believe that any of us would exchange places with any other people of any other generation. The energy, the faith, the devotion which we bring to this endeavor will light our country and all who serve it—and the glow from that fire can truly light the world.

Only the most skeptical Americans failed to be moved by Kennedy's (or Ted Sorenson's) stirring prose, but once

*Department of State Bulletin, August 23, 1954.

again, what was perhaps most notable about this celebrated pledge was that, fourteen years after the enuncia-
tion of the Truman Doctrine, at the beginning of a new
decade and a new administration, it repeated and ampli-
fied both the rhetoric and commitment to assume everywhere and at whatever cost "the survival and the success
of liberty." The crusade which had begun in the Balkans
had become global within fifteen years. It is curious and
significant to note that, since the conflict was most acute
there on Inauguration Day, 1961, the foreign country
which President Kennedy may have had foremost in his
mind when he uttered these ringing words was, of all
places, Laos.

As ambassador to Laos from 1954 to 1956 I can testify
that there is nowhere to be found a people more innocent
and more endearing, more attached to a peaceful and
unstrenuous life, more wantonly, lawlessly and brutally
attacked by their neighbors, than the Laotians. There can
be no question at all that the North Vietnamese, by
keeping "foreign forces" (their own) in Laos, violated the
Geneva Accord of 1954 almost before the ink was dry on
it; that they continued to violate it consistently in the same
way for eight years until a new accord was signed in 1962;
and that they then proceeded to violate the new one even
more flagrantly for another ten years. Therefore, on January 20, 1961, the freedom of Laos was, and still is today,
certainly at stake. However, there could be serious question about the conclusion drawn from this fact by succes-
sive U.S. administrations—that it was in the interests of
the Laotian people to be "defended" by the United States,
particularly by the American air force, no matter what the
cost, year after year after year, in villages destroyed, and in
people killed, maimed and made homeless. It is doubtful
that even the Truman, Kennedy or Nixon doctrines warrant destroying a people in order to "save" it.

This tragic example illustrates the extent to which the
justification for a monolithic anti-Communist ideology

has worn threadbare since the death of Stalin and particularly since the Sino-Soviet schism. As George Kennan
wrote a few years ago: "There is today no such thing as
'communism' in the sense that there was in 1947; there are
only a number of national regimes which cloak themselves
in verbal trappings of radical Marxism and follow domestic policies influenced to one degree or another by Marxist
concepts."*

It must not be imagined, however, by a generation of
Americans who grew up after the Cold War had somewhat
subsided that the American crusade had any other object
—in its origins, at least—than the containment of a postwar Soviet policy which could justly be described as
imperialism of the grossest kind; had we and our allies not
acted to contain it, it would certainly have spread the Iron
Curtain and the Brezhnev Doctrine over many more
nations than—thanks to our resistance—it was able to do.
To my generation this seems so obvious as to be hardly
worth repeating; to the newer one, apparently, it cannot be
repeated too often. Not, God knows, to keep alive old and
stale animosities but because, with the usual wild swing
of the pendulum of opinion, those who organized containment are now being called "war criminals," while those
who invaded South Korea in 1950 and Czechoslovakia in
1968 are still in power and show little sign of having
abated their theology or their ambitions.

The point made in this section, however, is the simple
and impartial one that the conduct of foreign affairs is
profoundly affected by ideologies, creeds and causes. Men
are so constituted that when they believe passionately in
the righteousness of their doctrines, they need only a taste
of power and a whiff of opportunity to induce them to
share these doctrines, by force of arms if necessary, with
the "unwitting masses" next door or even far away. And
since nothing proves one more right than victory, the more

*George Kennan, *op. cit.*

they win the more they want, until at last . . . "Those whom the gods wish to destroy they first make mad."

The Psychology of Leaders

There is an old argument between those, like Carlyle, who believe that history is primarily shaped by the will of "great men" and those, like Tolstoy, who believe that great men, like small ones, are swept along by a tide of events over which they have little or no control.

Even the Communists are of two minds on this point. On the one hand, they argue that the course of history is scientifically and inexorably determined by the principles of Marxism. On the other hand, they insist that *their* great men, such as Lenin and Mao, have by their genius and resolution seized opportunities to apply their principles in such a way as dramatically to hasten the march of history. It would be hard to deny this latter point, but the deification of Lenin and Mao probably reflects less a historical judgment than an emotional need to provide—in the absence of God, saints and prophets—surrogate figures for worship and inspiration. Certainly the enormous pictures of Lenin and Mao which one encounters in Russia and China, as well as at their embassies abroad, remind one of nothing so much as the great ikons of Czarist times or the bronze Buddhas of ancient China. (Incidentally, it is interesting to note how, whether or not in unconscious imitation of this Communist imagery, photographs of the incumbent American President, which were rarely encountered when I entered government service forty years ago, are now on almost mandatory display in every government office at home and abroad.)

On the basis of personal observation of the conduct of both domestic and foreign affairs over the past half century, I am also inclined to take an ambivalent view on whether "great men" can change or hasten history. Having in mind the extent to which the freedom of maneuver of a leader is circumscribed by such factors as the physical resources of his country, the deep-seated prejudices of his people, the power of pressure groups inside and outside government, the strength or weakness of neighbors and rivals, it is tempting to consider him as being more shuttlecock than battledore, more moved by events than moving them. On the other hand, it would be hard to deny that the character, temper, style and obsessions of leaders have at crucial times influenced, sometimes even determined, the course of history. Had Lenin not been leader of the small Bolshevik sect in Petrograd in 1917, it might well not have come to power—and if it had not, how different the world might be. Had there been no Adolf Hitler, it is hard to imagine that a party like the Nazis would have ever won office in Germany—or even if it had, that it would have behaved in office as it did. Who knows whether England could have held together in 1940 if Winston Churchill had not been there?

In any case, it is safe to say that the character and psychology of leaders is a significant factor in determining the conduct and misconduct of foreign affairs. René Dubos has remarked: "The power of the personal past is so great that it can distort the meaning of any event and magnify trivial happenings into momentous experiences. Human reactions are so profoundly influenced by the individual past that they are usually unpredictable and therefore appear completely irrational."*

It should be the first object of observers of statesmen to examine their personal past in order to try to perceive the compulsions that drive them and hence the directions in which they are likely to move. Instead, unfortunately, it is the habit of most observers, and indeed most participants

*René Dubos, *So Human an Animal* (New York: Charles Scribner's Sons, 1968).

in foreign affairs, to attribute the conduct of adversaries to original sin or false doctrine, the conduct of their own leaders to sober realism or purest principle, and the conduct of those who refuse to take sides to immorality or irresponsibility. Little serious effort is made to put oneself inside the skin of the adversary, or even of the ally, and to conceive from his point of view what his supposed interests are and how inimical or self-serving one's own policies may seem to him.

This is why we are again and again surprised both by the unforeseen and "irrational" behavior of our adversaries and by the irrelevance and ineffectiveness of much of what we do. It may therefore be useful to illustrate briefly from the history of the past four decades instances in which the personality of leaders has had a decisive or partial effect on events.

It is a shocking reflection on our era and our generation that the two leaders who have probably had the profoundest impact on human events in the past forty years, Hitler and Stalin, were both monsters. That is to say, both were men whose personal past had been, in ways we shall never fully know, so destructive of identity and balance that despite their undoubted genius they were profoundly psychotic. Yet both achieved total mastery of great nations and conducted single-handedly for many years the foreign affairs of those nations. One was more responsible than any other for bringing on World War II, the second for creating the Cold War; both callously, almost gleefully, slaughtered millions of human beings. Comparable examples of the domination of historical periods by single individuals, particularly diabolic individuals, are rare.

Hitler

Hitler embodied the frustrations, fantasies and nightmares of the lower middle class, "the silent majority" of Germans in the interwar period, a class whose national pride had been affronted by defeat and humiliation in 1918; whose economic security had twice been shattered by the devaluations of the early twenties and the depression of the late twenties; whose allegiance the Weimar Republic had never been able to win; and who were psychologically unprepared to partici- pate effectively in a democracy. Hitler rose from obscurity to total power in about four years by embodying, fusing and projecting the frustrations and fantasies of this group and by deluding the business and military establishment into providing essential initial support. Thereafter, for seven years (1935–42), he kept his adversaries off balance by the boldness and swiftness of his movements, and thus determined the course of European history.

Yet, as Albert Speer's recent autobiography has so graphically shown, Hitler's personal life was as mediocre and banal as that of the silent majority he represented and misled. His evenings with his chosen circle were as insipid and vacuous as those of Louis XIV or Queen Victoria—or, in a more boisterous and barbarous style, those of his counterpart, Stalin, as described by Khrush- chev and Djilas. The decisive elements of his personal history were probably his poverty-stricken, fatherless childhood, his insecure youth in a Vienna infected with anti-Semitism, his failure as an architect, his intoxication with German myth and mysticism (particularly as ex- pressed in the music of Wagner), and his ambivalent experience of exaltation and despair in World War I. Indeed, one might say that he was the most fateful casualty of that war, the Unknown Soldier who outlived his time and by his demonic genius reproduced it.

As Santayana said, those who do not learn from history are condemned to repeat it. In any case, the mistake of the Europeans between the two wars was that they learned little or nothing from the first one; victors and vanquished alike were still concerned twenty years later with pursuing the same parochial goals for which they had fought so bloodily and futilely. For that reason, until 1939 Hitler seemed to them just another German nationalist whom responsibility would sober and with whom conventional accommodations could be made. Very few outside Germany bothered to read *Mein Kampf*—or, if they did, believed it.

No doubt even fewer had read Edmund Burke, who in 1791 had written in a letter to a member of the French Assembly: "Society cannot exist unless a controlling power upon will and appetite be placed somewhere, and the less of it there is within, the more there must be without. It is ordained in the eternal constitution of things that men of intemperate minds cannot be free. Their passions forge their fetters."

Soviet Leaders

A fascinating book could and should be written on the psychology of Soviet leaders, since so much of modern history is a response to the challenge they posed or were thought to pose.

The personal past of Lenin influenced the whole future of the Communist movement. His dedication to revolution grew out of the oppressive environment of Czarist Russia, particularly the execution of his brother, and out of his enthrallment by the pseudo-scientific, seemingly rigorous doctrine of Marxism. He determined once and for all the character of the movement by his choice of a small, uncompromising, tightly disciplined, highly centralized sect, rather than an open democratic party, to lead the proletariat to socialism. Less novel but equally fateful was his decision to maintain by force and terror the dictatorship of the small sect after it came to power. The essential framework of Stalinism was created by Lenin and cannot be dissociated from him. The present rulers of all Communist countries rightly speak of Marxism-Leninism as their holy writ and regard Vladimir Ilyich as the father of their movement.

Stalin's role was to solidify and dominate the party and policy apparatus, and to use it with calculated brutality to control every aspect of both domestic and foreign affairs. His significant personal background was precisely his long, devious, silent and successful experience in building the party in his image and under his control, in eliminating by fraud or force all his rivals, and in rooting out or subjugating to the party all other elements in Soviet society. He was in a sense a madly logical *apparatchik,* a *bureaucrat à l'outrance.* His prescription for keeping the bureaucracy pure, subservient and diligent was periodically to decapitate it—literally and to a superabundant degree. This accorded with the most deep-seated of his personal characteristics: his cynical distrust of every other human being. Actually, he never believed in Marxism or Communism, but simply used them as he would have used Catholicism, Islam, Fascism or the military-industrial complex had he been born in another country.

Withal he was a man of extraordinary intellect and will. As suggested in pictures taken at the Potsdam Conference, in these respects he stood head and shoulders above his two partners there, Truman and Churchill. Indeed, in these respects I believe that he also stood above most of his prominent contemporaries, including Roosevelt, Hitler and De Gaulle, but not Mao.

Nevertheless, in foreign affairs Stalin was as prudent as he was cynical and rapacious. When the Soviet Union was weak (up until 1943) his foreign policy was extremely cautious and defensive. From 1944 to 1950, he seized what he safely could when opportunity offered, but even then he drew back from Iran, Greece, Turkey, Berlin and even Yugoslavia when expansion there became risky. I do not believe he would have endorsed the attack on South Korea—which he presumably anticipated would be a cheap gain if successful, and a means of further embroiling China and the United States if unsuccessful—had he foreseen it would lead to the rearmament of Germany. He was very far from being infallible. While making his country a superpower, his basic strategy has made it in the broadest sense less secure and more vulnerable than it was in 1945.

Stalin's successor, Khrushchev, was the most audacious and imaginative, the least rigid and doctrinaire, of Soviet leaders. He was vain, impulsive and highly emotional, swinging easily and abruptly from one posture to another, boldly conciliatory in foreign affairs if he thought it expedient, dangerously belligerent if he felt rebuffed or cornered. Arthur Miller's quip about the Russians—"I have never met cunning so naïve or naïveté so cunning"—often seemed to apply to him. Yet he had a fund of down-to-earth common sense rare in the heady upper air of political life. Once he had been convinced that nuclear war meant mutual annihilation—one of his graphic sayings was that "the living would envy the dead"—his first external priority came to be the avoidance of such a war. As suggested earlier, it is one of the great tragedies of the postwar period that an opportunity to deal seriously with Khrushchev to wind down the Cold War was missed by the West between 1958 and 1960. Likewise, despite his conspicuous shortcomings, it was a loss to his country and the world when he was ousted from power in 1964.

If Stalin was the mad bureaucrat, it almost seems that Khrushchev's successors are bureaucrats who have been programmed and automated. Their objects seem to be to stay firmly on top of every aspect of Soviet life; to keep the machinery running along the most conventional lines; to treat armaments as the most precious of status symbols and pyramid them higher and higher at whatever cost; and to take advantage of external opportunities only with carefully calculated circumspection. Admittedly, after one has been governing for twenty or thirty years, for the most part under the baleful eye of a Stalin or a Khrushchev, one's capacity for intellectual and moral initiative is likely to be attenuated. There is certainly nothing diabolic about the present Soviet leadership, but it is undoubtedly the most conservative of that of any great power.

One wonders how, for all its rockets and secret agents, such a leadership can possibly cope with the technological and political imperatives of the next twenty years. The fact that these leaders are holding summit meetings with the Americans to check the useless multiplication of nuclear weapons and avidly seeking technology from the West shows they are aware there are problems. But they continue to rely on only the most cautious and conventional of "solutions," and most constricting of all, to keep intact their medieval police apparatus and thought control. The Soviet Union has a planned economy, but its plans are fundamentally out of date. The framework for them was laid down a hundred years ago by Marx (on premises that have since been shown to be palpably false), articulated loosely and pragmatically by Lenin, but frozen into concrete by Stalin forty years ago for purposes of political control rather than economic efficiency. And so they remain today despite all the vague chatter about "reform."

When Lincoln Steffens visited Russia in 1919 he said: "I have been over into the future and it works": Now, after a visit to the Soviet Union, one is tempted to say, "I have been over into the past. How much longer can it hold together?" There is some pertinence in the question posed by Andrei Amalrik, a young Soviet dissident now exiled in Siberia: "Will the Soviet Union survive until 1984?" No doubt it will, but in what shape?

Still, one must never forget that except in times of great catastrophe, the Russian people are themselves deeply conservative, and the present leadership may be just what "the silent majority" wants. To quote Arthur Miller once more: "Even people who see clearly that all is not well seem to desire that this same pyramidal structure remain undisturbed. It is as though there were an anarchy in the center of their beings which, if left to itself, would expand

to a dematerialization of all order." It may be many years
before the technological demands of a modern economy
become so imperative that they overcome this innate
Russian conservatism and dread of the nihilism in its own
soul.

Mao Tse-tung

Because China has been more
or less encapsulated for
twenty years, dimly mis-
perceived only through the eyes of enemies or venerators,
we have hardly begun to measure the influence of Mao
Tse-tung on his country and his time. As to the former, it
certainly equals and probably surpasses that of Lenin on
his country or Gandhi on his; as to the latter, it may be that
like most religious leaders his impact on the future will be
greater than on his own. His impact on the philosophy and
behavior of the largest community of mankind is already
stronger than that of any predecessor during the past
millennium. His impact may be even greater on the
universal history of the era into which we are just moving
and to which his austere and egalitarian gospel may prove
to be particularly congenial.

Mao is truly what is so rarely found in history—both a
sincere and successful revolutionary and the founder of a
church. His deliberately unstable but consistent system of
government, if one can call it that, is best epitomized in
one of his own sayings: "Everyone on a horse's back must
be brought down once in a while to share the burdens of
the long march as a corrective to one's soul and behavior."

It would be difficult to exaggerate the effect on the
psychology of the Chinese Communists, and hence on
modern Chinese history, of the Long March of six thousand miles they endured in 1934, and the following years
of embattled isolation in the badlands of Yenan. In those
times they developed the practice of fraternity among
themselves and with the peasants, the habit of austerity
and shared self-denial, which bent and recast both the

alien dogma of Marx and the traditional pragmatism of China.

The essence of Mao's doctrine is that by "right thinking" the common man can work miracles, but that he is easily corrupted by love of power and place, the sins of sloth and the flesh. Therefore Mao has written and spread far and wide his "little red book"; therefore, in the Great Leap Forward and the Cultural Revolution, he has twice stripped the fattening bureaucrats of perquisites and power, shattered the molds of his own revolution and commanded the impossible of the common man.

Such a "system" could have lasted as long as it has only through the extraordinary abilities of some of Mao's coadjutors—most of all, Chou En-lai—and through the remarkable steadfastness, patience and diligence of the Chinese people. For the third time they are now rebuilding their society, their infrastructure and their elite after Mao has brought them down from the "horse's back." Mao and Chou, inspired by fear of their Marxist and national rival, the Soviet Union, are even breaking bread and exchanging bland and ambiguous toasts with the American "imperialists" they so long denounced.

It is generally supposed that the reign of the living Mao Tse-tung is almost over. He cannot live forever, nor can Chou and the other survivors of the Long March. No one can be sure who or what will follow. No crystal ball is more clouded. The military were called in to end the disorders of the Cultural Revolution, but after the purging of their leader, Lin Piao, their future, too, is uncertain. Perhaps the party bureaucracy will revive, refreshed by brainwashing, and preserve the harmony and progress which now seems to prevail. Perhaps when Mao and Chou die, everything will fall apart again into the anarchy that characterizes China between dynasties. The greatest weakness of dictatorships, including Communist ones, is their lack of provision for legitimate and uncontested succession.

From a more philosophic viewpoint, it is not as certain as most seem to suppose that traditional Chinese pragmatism will triumph soon and easily even over the dead Mao. It would be rash to try to predict the life span of his *Thoughts* or of the Marxist-Christian-Confucian elixir with which he may have inculcated not only China but a rejuvenated Orient. Certainly those both in West and East who will be conducting foreign affairs with China over the next few decades should read and ponder the *Thoughts of Mao,* as earlier generations of statesmen would have saved themselves much anguish had they taken account of the tedious works of Mohammed, Marx and Hitler.

American Leaders
ROOSEVELT

Franklin Roosevelt was that rare combination—a guileful man with a heart. This combination accounted for his enormous success at home in leading his country out of the depression, away from unadulterated "free enterprise" and toward the mixed and more humane economic system of the future.

In foreign affairs Roosevelt was usually right about the great issues. However objectionable the Soviet regime might be, he saw that a serious and persistent effort must be made to get along with its leaders if peace was to be preserved after the war. He saw that the era of European colonialism was drawing to a close and that the peoples of Asia and Africa must soon be accorded the liberty and self-determination for which two great wars had ostensibly been fought. He saw that the United States must deal with the nations of Latin America as equals and friends. He saw that a new international organization, stronger than the League of Nations, was required to keep the peace, and that its success would depend on some measure of cooperation among the great powers, including the Soviet Union and China.

On the other hand, Roosevelt had little or no experience

in foreign affairs before he became President, and his conduct of them demonstrated his inexperience. First, with excessive self-confidence he assumed far too much of the burden himself; hence, lacking expert advice, he made frequent mistakes of tactics and in the end wore out both himself and his one trusted adjutant, Harry Hopkins. He imagined that he could cajole or beguile powerful leaders of origins and outlooks wholly different from his own— Stalin, Chiang Kai-shek or De Gaulle—as if they were American politicians. He appointed and tolerated for eleven and a half years an inadequate Secretary of State, and used the Secretary's shortcomings as an excuse for indulging his own preference for carrying on foreign policy, in cavalier disregard of his department of foreign affairs.

Contrarily, as a lifelong naval buff, Roosevelt had considerable regard for the military, and fell easy prey to their oversimplified thesis that politics must not be allowed to interfere with "winning the war," and that political decisions must be adjourned till the war was over. This was a mistake no other major wartime leader—Churchill, Stalin, De Gaulle or Chiang—would have dreamed of making, and it seriously aggravated the problems Roosevelt's successors had to confront. Moreover, his introduction of the military into the center of foreign policy decision-making in wartime established a practice wholly foreign to American tradition. When this practice was carried over by his successors into peacetime, a strong and often unhealthy military bias was injected into decision-making through the next three decades. Had he appointed Henry Stimson Secretary of State instead of Secretary of War in 1940, the course of subsequent history might have been rather different.

In foreign affairs Roosevelt's judgment on the basic issues was sound and prescient, and therefore he was successful in his lifetime, but his administration of these affairs was amateurish and faulty, resulting in grave errors, some of which his successors have corrected but many of which they have continued or even compounded.

TRUMAN   Truman was even less pre-
                           pared for the conduct of for-
                           eign affairs than Roosevelt,
but he took advice. He appointed successively as Secretary
of State three men of wide experience, James Byrnes,
Marshall and Acheson, and equally important, gave them
latitude and accepted their counsel. In turn, these men
organized the formulation and conduct of foreign policy
in an imaginative, coordinated and efficient manner. As a
result, between 1947 and 1950 new policies and new
instruments appropriate to the new postwar environment—the Truman Doctrine, the Marshall Plan, NATO
and the UN's resistance to aggression in Korea—were
rapidly devised and applied. There has probably been no
period in American history when the conduct of foreign
affairs was both so significant and so successful, and
Truman deserves great credit for presiding over it.

On the other hand, Truman was more impulsive than
sagacious. An understandable sense of insecurity following his sudden accession to enormous power—an apprehension that more experienced and unscrupulous operators like Stalin would try to push him around—reinforced
his natural propensity and sometimes caused him to
overreact. This showed itself clearly, for example, during
his first tragicomic conversation with Molotov only ten
days after he took office, as well as on a number of
occasions at Potsdam. This insecurity may have contributed to the open-ended character of the Truman Doctrine as it finally emerged and to the extravagant conclusions about Soviet intentions drawn from the attack on
South Korea. These shortcomings played their part in
leading this President into the internal and external im-
passe which aborted the last two years of his administration.

Truman and his counselors had the wit and courage to respond effectively and imaginatively to the Soviet challenge in Europe and Asia in the years immediately after the war. However, by the beginning of 1947, less than a year and a half after V-J Day, they had given up any serious effort to prolong any semblance of the wartime accommodation and association because they believed the Soviets were implacably determined not only to maintain their system where it was established but to extend it further wherever opportunity offered.

Certainly in the previous two years Stalin had given substantial grounds for such a belief. In addition to the progressive takeover of Eastern Europe and threats elsewhere, there was the outrageous tone of Soviet discourse. I can well remember how, as a staff member of our delegation to the UN General Assembly in the fall of 1946, we were at first dismayed and then infuriated by the violence of Vishinsky's attacks upon the United States, to which by the end of the session we were, not unnaturally, responding in kind.

Nevertheless, it is not clear in retrospect that the Communist threat in 1947 was so universal and so imminent as Truman and his advisers imagined, or that, such as it was, it might not have been to some modest degree mitigated by more painstaking and patient efforts at conciliation along with the necessary measures of deterrence and containment. Perhaps, as we look back with the benefit of hindsight, it is a pity that Dewey did not win in 1948. A considerable proportion of the hard-line gestures and rhetoric of the Truman Administration were designed to forestall attacks by the Republicans, embittered and frantic, as noted earlier, by their long divorce from power. Had they won in 1948, they might have been better able and more willing to prevent the Cold War from becoming quite as savage as it did. At least the country might have been spared McCarthy.

But then we should also have missed Dean Acheson as

Secretary of State. I have no hesitation in putting him at the top of the list of the ten Secretaries under whom I have served. In his grasp of the essentials of enormously complicated situations, in his clarity and eloquence in presenting them, in his open-mindedness toward conflicting views, in the breadth of his wisdom and erudition, in the gaiety and penetration of his humor, in the warmth and humanity of his personality, he was—at least when I knew him as Assistant Secretary, Undersecretary and in his first two years as Secretary—unequaled. Subsequently he was so slandered and hounded that his temper soured, and in a curious and uncharacteristic reaction, he became, on some issues, more reactionary than some of his critics. But that was after he left office, and as happens to most of us, his arteries hardened.

EISENHOWER AND DULLES   By the time Eisenhower came
to office the pattern of the
Cold War was firmly established and, even with the best will in the world, would have been hard to alter. Almost simultaneously, Stalin died, which at least created opportunities worth exploring.

Remarkably enough for a lifelong soldier, Eisenhower was temperamentally a man of peace, instinctively humane and sympathetic to his fellow-men, inclined to be skeptical of military adventures and military solutions. He brought the Korean War to an end and kept his country out of Vietnam in 1954 despite the prodding of his Vice-President and Secretary of State. Partly because of his wariness and sense of sound administration, partly because of John Foster Dulles' strong character, the Joint Chiefs of Staff in his time were rarely allowed to get out of bounds. His last act in office (somewhat reminiscent of Lenin's deathbed warning about Stalin) was to alert the nation to the excessive power of the military-industrial complex.

At the same time Eisenhower was not notable for

profundity or vigor of intellect. He had only the most nebulous and bland of political philosophies. His great successes had been achieved as conciliator rather than initiator. Except for brief moments of irascibility, he was easygoing and preferred to drift along with an uneasy but tolerable situation rather than to make an effort to improve it radically. Because of his temperament and military background he relied heavily on his staff, his senior advisers, and in most cases he followed their advice as long as they stayed within their respective bailiwicks and did not risk getting him into serious trouble at home or abroad.

This predisposition of his chief, as much as his own strength of character and political astuteness, accounted for the remarkable authority exercised by Dulles. His indomitable vigor of will prevented any encroachment by others, military or civilian, on his chosen field and enabled him to dominate the conduct of U.S. foreign policy for six years. As has often been noted, he was first of all a Presbyterian, a Calvinist in almost every aspect of his life, except in his fondness for good food and rye whiskey. He had no doubt that he was chosen to lead the good fight against the forces of evil—in his case, "world Communism." He had not an iota of respect, understanding or charity for men who led that "wicked" movement, and he was prepared to use any means or instruments available to fight it. These included a use of the military and the CIA going well beyond ordinary conceptions of public morality.

Dulles was doubtful, at times contemptuous, of even close allies who did not fully share his single-minded convictions, particularly if they weakened the common front by pursuing what seemed to him secondary national interests, as for example the British and French at Suez in 1956. As a lawyer he was perhaps unduly impressed with pacts and treaties, though he usually saw to it they were worded so as not to bind him excessively. He was often accused of hypocrisy, but this was only because he displayed, rather more conspicuously than most, a conviction common to many statesmen that ends justify means, and because he tended to be publicly pious about both.

At the same time, probably as a result of his personal observation of the disastrous veto of the League of Nations by the U.S. Senate, Dulles was extremely sensitive to public and particularly Congressional opinion. This led him, on the one hand, to a rather craven compliance with McCarthy's witch hunting, with disastrous effects on the morale of his Department; on the other hand, however, it assured a steady and fruitful collaboration between executive and legislative branches on foreign issues throughout the tenure of his office. As to his conduct of his Department, he worked for the most part with a very small group of advisers and disliked and neglected administration, but he appointed to most of the senior posts at home and abroad career Foreign Service officers, whom he found to be reliable and sophisticated executors of his policies.

I knew Mr. Dulles well and have the most congenial recollection of him. I recall him as a delegate to the UN Assembly in 1946 trying indefatigably but in vain to reach some accommodation with the Soviets about the UN trusteeship system. I remember him as a Republican adviser at the meeting of Foreign Ministers in Paris in 1949 protesting against what seemed to him our disposition always to react against Soviet initiatives rather than to undertake initiatives ourselves which would cause them trouble in Central or Eastern Europe. On the visit to Laos referred to in the first section of this book I recall his patiently calling separately on each of the four chief personalities of this frail government, because I had advised him that no one of them would speak frankly in the presence of the others. I remember him in Paris shortly after the Suez crisis engaging in a polite but cold dialogue of the deaf with Premier Guy Mollet. I recall him vividly in Washington assembling and hurling his thunderbolts at the time of the Iraqi coup and our landing in Lebanon in

1958, less than a year before he died. I was far from agreeing with all of these or others of his policies, but I never doubted for a moment in his time that American foreign policy was directed by a strong will, an acute intelligence and a dauntless spirit.

KENNEDY   It is not easy for me to appraise John Fitzgerald Kennedy objectively because I shared with tens of millions of human beings, young and old, Americans, Europeans, Asians, Africans, a susceptibility to his charisma. When he came to office, people everywhere were refreshed and inspired, as though setting sail at the dawn of a bright new day with youth at the helm. At last, after years of stagnation, we were going places. Everything seemed possible, and only the best probable.

His gaiety, candor and wit charmed even cynical journalists at press conferences. It was clearly his intention not to tell the people as little as he could get away with, but as much as he felt he possibly could. Despite his wealth, he was an instinctive democrat. Most exciting of all was his receptivity to new ideas; most reassuring his simplicity, unpretentiousness and human decency. Yet when he entered a meeting—whether in the Cabinet Room of the White House or in Madison Square Garden—one had no doubt that here was a leader, not one who was either overbearing or sly or unsure of himself, but one with a conscience, a will and a heart.

Unfortunately, Kennedy did not have enough time, or perhaps enough audacity, to achieve much in a thousand days. Woodrow Wilson, for example, accomplished more between 1913 and 1915 with a still narrower margin of popular support. When Kennedy came to office, his youth, while a moral and political asset, was also a handicap in that he had no experience in any executive capacity or in the conduct of foreign policy. Lack of experience, youth and the narrowness of his electoral victory may have impressed him to an unfortunate degree in the opening months of his administration with a sense of being on trial. This was reflected both in a certain diffidence, for example, in his reluctance to call off the long-prepared but disastrous Bay of Pigs operation, and, like Truman, in his determination to show that he could not be "pushed around," as in his posture vis-à-vis the Soviets in 1961–62.

Moreover, Kennedy's wartime experience gave him a kind of taste for military dispositions and solutions. This inclination was aggravated by his electoral commitment to overcome the "missile gap" (subsequently found to be nonexistent). He therefore presided over an enormous buildup of U.S. strategic and conventional military forces. This buildup, coupled with their humiliating defeat in the Cuban crisis, goaded the Soviets on their part into undertaking an equally enormous and unnecessary response which is still going on. The United States would probably be more secure if Kennedy had never added a single missile, submarine or soldier to those programmed before he took office.

In offering response to challenge over the last twenty-five years, both American and Soviet leaders have often forgotten the elementary fact that response not only provokes counter-response, but also sometimes creates challenges where they did not exist before or did not exist to the same degree. On the other hand, when there actually was an acute danger of nuclear war arising from the Cuban crisis, Kennedy acted with admirable restraint and rejected the reckless advice of his military staff to bomb or invade Cuba.

His military predispositions also led Kennedy and his brother Robert to embrace with undiscriminating enthusiasm the fashionable pursuit of "counterinsurgency." This was a technique required in principle to cope with Communist insurgency, but it was grafted onto the U.S. military establishment primarily in order to give the

ground forces, which felt left out of the strategic competition, a "slice of the action." It reflected two naïve presumptuous beliefs: first, that the United States had an
obligation to help cope with Communist insurgency
wherever it occurred; and second, that soldiers from
Georgia, Iowa and Oregon could better cope with insurgency in environments wholly alien to them than could
the natives of those environments.

Kennedy was ambivalent about Vietnam and Laos. On
the one hand, he understood intellectually, and several
times stated, that in the last analysis only the people of
those countries could preserve their own independence; if
they had not the will, we could not do it for them. On the
other hand, he was saddled with the commitments of the
past fifteen years: the Truman Doctrine, SEATO and
substantial U.S. political, military and economic involvement in the two countries. More important still, he shared
the ultimate nightmare of every postwar American President, conjured up in large part by Joe McCarthy: the fear
of being held responsible for "losing" another country to
Communism. The evangelist Billy Graham quotes him as
saying, after a golf game just before his inauguration in
January 1961: "We cannot allow Laos and South Vietnam
to fall to the Communists."* And like the whole Kennedy
clan, he was brought up to play to win.

It is impossible to say precisely what Kennedy would
have done about Vietnam had he lived. It is unlikely that
he would have pulled out or allowed himself to be thrown
out. Nevertheless, he would probably have had the wit not
to let himself and his country become so massively involved, and would have made a far more serious effort
than Johnson or Nixon did to negotiate a settlement, even
at the cost, as in the Laos Accord of 1962, of substantial
concessions.

In the actual conduct of foreign affairs, Kennedy, like

The New York Times, April 9, 1971.

Roosevelt, tended to be contemptuous of the State Department and the Foreign Service, perhaps in part because of his experiences in the London embassy in his youth, because of their loyal execution of Republican policies under Dulles, or because of his impatience with any executive bureaucracy. He was by nature an activist, disposed to vigorous movement rather than cautious calculation. He was scornful of what seemed to him lethargy, timidity or standpattism on the part of the State Department. Sometimes he was right, but more often it was when he was being compulsively gung-ho that he got himself and the country into trouble.

Kennedy revived the ill-fated practice of Wilson and FDR of trying to be his own Secretary of State, but he carried much further than they did the creation inside the White House of a duplicate foreign office under a brilliant and vigorous Security Affairs adviser, McGeorge Bundy. On this point, one might note Dean Acheson's pithy comment: "The President cannot be Secretary of State; it is inherently impossible in the nature of both positions. What he can do, and often has done with unhappy results, is to prevent anyone else from being Secretary of State."*

Still, Kennedy was a leader of great luster and promise. In foreign affairs he made serious mistakes which misled and bedeviled his more doctrinaire successors. He himself, however, had he lived, might have corrected them. He was growing fast at the time of his death. The contrast between his Inaugural Address and his American University speech in June 1963 is remarkable.

In the latter he said, for example, that if world war should come again, all that Americans and Russians had built, "all we have worked for, would be destroyed in the first twenty-four hours. . . . We are both caught up in a vicious and dangerous cycle in which suspicion on one

---

*Dean Acheson, *Present at the Creation* (New York: W. W. Norton, 1969), p. 88.

side breeds suspicion on the other, and new weapons beget counterweapons. . . . If we cannot end now all our differences, at least we can help make the world safe for diversity. For, in the final analysis, our most basic common link is that we all inhabit this small planet. We all breathe the same air. We all cherish our children's future. And we are all mortal."*

It was a tragedy for his country and the world that John Kennedy died when he did. Had he lived and been reelected, he would have become an extraordinary, perhaps even a great, President.

STEVENSON   While in his speeches he had much to say that was wise and uplifting about foreign policy, Adlai Stevenson never conducted foreign affairs except in a subordinate and controlled capacity. This was a tragedy. While the two might often have clashed and the relationship might not have lasted long, had Kennedy made him Secretary of State, the President and the country would probably have been spared some of the more egregious errors that were made.

There was a myth propagated by men who thought themselves practical that Stevenson was too idealistic, naïve and indecisive to be successful or even safe in high office. The fact is that there is no one more naïve or unrealistic than a hard-liner. To intimidate or cow an adversary, he is constantly calling for strong action, which if it were applied against himself would provoke him to the most outraged and violent reaction. Yet it never seems to occur to such people that the adversary will, unless he is so weak as to be negligible, react in exactly the same way that they would, and that the collision of two reckless displays of "strength" is likely to produce at best a

*Arthur Schlesinger, *A Thousand Days* (Boston: Houghton Mifflin, 1965).

fruitless standoff, at worst a common catastrophe. The fact is that hard-liners are usually people who, for all their bluster, are unsure of themselves. They are so desperately afraid of seeming weak that they furiously reject all those compromises and accommodations which are the stuff of international stability and peace.

If Adlai Stevenson had been Secretary of State and had been listened to, there would have been no Bay of Pigs. The withdrawal of Soviet missiles from Cuba would have been accompanied by the withdrawal of U.S. missiles from Turkey, which had previously been decided but which, if ostensibly tied to the Soviet withdrawal from Cuba, would have saved Soviet face, might have prolonged Khrushchev's tenure of power, and might not have provoked the subsequent massive Soviet strategic and naval expansion which now confronts us. As to Vietnam, while Stevenson felt and spoke strongly against Communist exploitation of "wars of national liberation" in Indochina and elsewhere, he was acutely aware that nationalism was at least as strong a factor as Communism in Vietnam, and he constantly pleaded for an indefatigable exploration of every chance of negotiation. One of the deepest frustrations of his last year was the self-righteous disregard by the Johnson Administration of a proposal for a meeting with the North Vietnamese in Rangoon which U Thant believed he had arranged.

In a sense, the appointment of Adlai Stevenson as U.S. Ambassador to the United Nations was cruel and unusual punishment. He was a dedicated believer in the United Nations and, while quite aware of its present shortcomings, had no doubt that in the long run it represented the shape of things to come. Since he could not be Secretary of State, he welcomed the opportunity to work in it, for it and through it for the goals of international understanding and human brotherhood in which he so deeply believed. Therefore it was particularly painful to see him obliged by his position and instructions to defend, on this most conspicuous of all world stages, such exercises in power politics as the Bay of Pigs, the Dominican operation, the exclusion of Communist China, support of South Africa and Portugal, and the bombing of North Vietnam. One sometimes had the impression of watching an elephant made to perform silly tricks in a circus ring. By the time of his death, the ambivalence and frustration these distasteful assignments engendered had largely destroyed his pleasure and pride in the job.

There was indeed an element of heroic naïveté in the foreign policy of Wilson, Roosevelt and Stevenson, but it was precisely their synthesis of vision and common sense which will cause them to be remembered long after their critics are forgotten, and which, had they been heeded, would have produced a better and safer world.

JOHNSON   In many ways Lyndon Johnson is a deeply tragic figure. A lifelong liberal, a Southerner who did more to establish civil rights for blacks than any other President, a man of compassion and goodwill whose greatest ambition was to be remembered as a bold domestic reformer, as the architect of the Great Society, he seems likely to go down in history chiefly as the President who led his country by guile and deceit into an unjust and unnecessary war, and was so discredited thereby that he dared not run for a second term. This is unfair. Johnson's infirmity was a very real naïveté; he was the first and most fatally to be beguiled and deluded.

Johnson's whole political experience before 1961 had been in Congress, where as Majority Leader of the Senate for many years he achieved remarkable success by what was known as "wheeling and dealing"—that is, a combination of trading, cajolery and browbeating, almost always behind closed doors. He certainly thought of himself as a man profoundly committed to peace, but as a Southerner and a Texan he had a particular dread of seeming weak and was therefore temperamentally inclined to react violently to whatever struck him as an attempt to intimidate or humiliate him and his country.

In foreign affairs Johnson had almost no direct experience, and for the most part he accepted unquestioningly the "conventional wisdom" of his day. He was therefore more than most at the mercy of civilian and military "experts" who interpreted and applied that "wisdom" for him and whose advice he, often reluctantly but almost invariably, followed. Moreover, his civilian advisers in foreign affairs were not, for the most part, experienced Foreign Service officers or even politicians but men brought by Kennedy into the White House and Defense and State Departments from the universities and from business.

Since it supplied the doctrine, one must sadly admit that the liberal intellectual establishment, as represented in government by some of its most brilliant and articulate members, bears a large share of the responsibility for Johnson's disastrous Vietnam policy from 1964 to 1968. Through the critical months of 1964 and early 1965, when it seemed likely that the feeble government in Saigon would collapse without massive American assistance, it should have been the obligation of these men to reexamine with the utmost rigor the underlying assumptions of U.S. policy toward Southeast Asia; they should have weighed with the utmost coolness and objectivity the disadvantages of withdrawing from Vietnam while our commitment was still relatively small, as opposed to the penalties of assuming the main burden of fighting a civil war in Asia against a sophisticated enemy who had already defeated the French. On the contrary, as the Pentagon Papers confirm, Johnson's gifted intellectual establishment never faced up to this choice at all—or at least never presented it dispassionately to the President. Instead they *assumed* that the U.S. could not tolerate the "loss" of Vietnam, and the debate was merely on how much the

U.S. should "insist" the Saigon government should do—most of which, of course, it never did—and on how much the U.S. itself would "have to do." Instant military reactions to the Tonkin Gulf episode in August 1964 and the Pleiku attack in February 1965 were merely the reflection of fundamental decisions implicitly taken earlier without sufficiently serious examination of either alternatives or consequences.

The professional military establishment was equally guilty of misleading a President unsophisticated in their business. The Chiefs of Staff may properly be charged with at least the following gross military and political miscalculations. They were eager to display jointly and separately the prowess of their respective services, but were seemingly unconscious of the ineptitude for this kind of war of their services as they were in 1965 constituted, armed and trained. They were unable to conceive that they could not defeat a contemptibly small and ill-equipped Asian adversary, and hence they constantly deceived the President and themselves with loaded reports of enemy casualties and with foolishly optimistic predictions of early victory. They were almost totally ignorant of the military and political realities of guerrilla warfare, and hence were mistaken again and again in their strategy and tactics. In their frustration when they could not prevail they constantly demanded more and more troops; yet they were constrained from using on the battlefield more than a small fraction of those they had because of a military system long afflicted with obesity in the wrong places. Finally, they devastated countless villages, killed more friends than enemies in the South and substantially reinforced morale in the North by an extravagant, counterproductive and incredibly callous use of air power.

In short, while Johnson as President had to bear the final responsibility, his disastrous policy in Vietnam and its even more disastrous repercussions at home and abroad grew out of an indiscriminate application, recommended by almost all his civil and military advisers, of long-standing policies to a new and inappropriate situation. To be sure, Johnson's personal style in the conduct of foreign policy also played a substantial part in the debacle. Aspects of this style were his habit of consulting seriously only a small group of advisers; his neglect of the Foreign Service establishment, including most of those with experience in Southeast Asia; his intolerance and disregard of opposing views; his fantastic deviousness and absence of candor with Congress, the public and even most of his subordinates; his lack of a "decent respect for the opinions of mankind"; and perhaps most of all, the extent to which he stubbornly came to subordinate most of the foreign and domestic policies of the United States to success in what should never have been more than a very minor theater of U.S. operations.

Yet it bears repeating that Johnson was of all the Americans deceived about Vietnam the most grossly and inexcusably deceived. One must in fairness conclude that nothing became him so much as the manner of his going.

NIXON   In the first year of his Administration the cartoonists had great sport contrasting what they called "the old Nixon" and "the new Nixon." Actually there was more truth than fancy in this conceit.

Richard Nixon's personal history was that of a young man of modest origins, with great persistence of will, strong but usually controlled emotions, and views of the world so conventional as to be almost a travesty, yet so homespun as to strike a sympathetic chord in many Americans. Perhaps because of his background, he seemed to have a latent sense of insecurity, under stress even taking the form of a persecution complex, as reflected in his outburst against the press after his defeat for the California governorship in 1962, or in his gratuitous assertion at the time of the invasion of Cambodia that he would not permit the United States to be treated as a "pitiful helpless giant."

With this background and temperament, Nixon clawed his way to the top in politics in remarkably short order, partly through the good fortune of being the right man in the right place, partly through seizing upon and exploiting ruthlessly at a psychological moment the issue of anti-Communism. Another facility, which he possessed despite his conventional views and which repeatedly stood him in good stead, was what could be described, depending on your point of view, either as pragmatism or as opportunism—in any case, a willingness to change horses in midstream with great agility: to abandon without a murmur or an excuse a position he had long and passionately held but which was proving politically inexpedient, and to switch blandly to a position he had long and passionately denounced. Obvious examples of this useful talent are his dramatic rapprochement with Communist China and his sudden conversion in August 1971 to a wage-price freeze which for two years he had been insisting was incompatible in peacetime with a free-enterprise system.

President Nixon's views on foreign affairs were no doubt indelibly imprinted during the teething years of the Cold War and were thereafter held with almost religious tenacity. Essentially he has seen the Soviet Union as the enemy of mankind, to be fought anywhere and everywhere with whatever weapons seemed effective. The fact that he wished to insert U.S. military forces in Vietnam in 1954, while he was Vice-President, is well known. While in that office he traveled to many countries, engaged in his "kitchen" debate with Khrushchev in Moscow and came to consider himself an expert on foreign affairs, though in my experience, brief ceremonial visits of this kind do little more than confirm the biases of the official visitor.

Nixon's defeat in the Presidential election of 1960 and

in California two years later no doubt left deep scars, but they also probably induced a fundamental personal reexamination—certainly not of his creed, but of the tactics for obtaining and holding power in the sixties and seventies which, as an intelligent man, he recognized were no longer the same as in the forties and fifties. His penchant for "pragmatism," for subordinating dogma to reality when politics so required, has lubricated and limbered his tactics. Thus "the new Nixon" was born, conducted the campaign of 1968, was elected, and proclaimed in his Inaugural Address that an era of negotiation had succeeded the era of confrontation.

The trouble is that a man cannot bury his past, and that the persistent and unquenchable "old Nixon" kept rudely shoving the new one aside in both domestic and foreign affairs. In 1968 he promised "to bring us together," and indeed there was a golden opportunity to do so, for after the bitter disputes and disorders they had just endured, the American people were more than ready to "lower their voices" and "move forward together." Yet—almost compulsively, it seemed—the President prolonged and extended the Indochina war, denounced the younger generation, neglected the blacks and unleashed a divisive and scurrilous Vice-President. His schoolboy belief that free enterprise if left to itself—with, of course, appropriate subsidies to business interests—would solve the economic problems of late twentieth-century technological society vitiated much of his domestic program, until he became convinced in the summer of 1971 that strict adherence to this maxim would cost him the 1972 election.

While Nixon repeatedly demanded of Americans and foreigners alike "respect for the Presidency," neither his unpredictable behavior nor his introverted style has done much to promote public trust. While he and his entourage denounced their critics in Congress and the press, they built a wall of silence or bombast between other legitimate representatives of the people and the solitary man bent over the yellow pad at Camp David.

The threat of "world Communism," centered in the Soviet Union, looms as large as ever in the back of Nixon's mind, but he has sought to deal with it in terms that are more subtle and more relevant to the 1970's. He deserves great credit for negotiating the first limits on the strategic arms race, though he still seems bent on developing new weapons systems while he circumscribes old ones. His broader pursuit of a more rational relationship with the Soviet Union is also admirable, but it suffers, as so often his policies do, from a curious ambivalence: simultaneously an insistent "linkage" of confrontations and differences all over the world and an extravagant plan for management of the world by those strange bedfellows, the two superpowers.

The President's reestablishment of contact and communication with Communist China, which he had bitterly opposed so long, was a rational and valuable step. His own visit there, his personal meeting with Mao, dramatized and sanctioned for both the American and the Chinese peoples, both so long misled about each other, the breaking of the twenty-year quarantine. Still, if one probed behind the TV screen and the fulsome toasts, the whole affair seemed more a spectacular move on the checkerboard of balance of power with the Soviets than an act of genuine statesmanship which took a wider world into account.

In his preoccupation with playing the superpower game Nixon gravely affronted such allies and friends as Europe, Japan and India, and seems remarkably willing to risk unraveling old alliances without weaving new ones of comparable reliability. He has withdrawn U.S. forces from Vietnam at a deliberate pace over four long years so that our client government in Saigon might at all costs be preserved until after the U.S. elections in 1972. When this goal—and incidentally his own reelection—seemed threatened by the North Vietnamese offensive in April 1972, he resumed the massive bombing of the North and mined Haiphong at grave risk of aborting accommodations with both the Soviet Union and China. Fortunately, the Soviets had invested too much in the Moscow summit to cancel it, but Nixon's gamble was nonetheless a reckless one, particularly since it seemed to have no real purpose aside from saving time and face for himself.

As this is written, the duration of the Vietnam war is still in doubt but its ultimate outcome is not. Even the President seems at last to have become aware of the decisive fact—that the patience of the Vietnamese is inexhaustible, but in a war not involving their vital interests, that of the Americans is not. How many deaths, how much agony and devastation, might have been spared both sides if the President had accepted this fact in 1969 instead of 1972.

So, as it has turned out, there is not too much difference between the old Nixon and the new one except in style and rhetoric. The new Nixon has undertaken bold departures from tired policies, but the old one took countervailing steps which often stalled the new departures. The distinction seems to be that in the old Nixon the disparity between the public and the private figure was small; in the new Nixon it is large.

On the basis of this cursory glimpse of the character and psychology of these leaders of the superpowers, is it possible to draw any conclusions about the relative weight of their contribution, as compared with that of impersonal factors, in determining the history of their time? Would the state of international relations in the 1970's be substantially different if Stalin had died in 1944, if Khrushchev had held on to power longer, if Kennedy had survived Oswald's bullets, if Dewey had been elected President rather than Truman, Stevenson rather than Eisenhower, Humphrey rather than Nixon?

Any response to what Roosevelt used to call "iffy" questions of this kind has to be highly speculative. There can be no doubt that certain leaders—Lenin, Hitler, Stalin, Mao, Gandhi, Roosevelt, Churchill, De Gaulle—substantially influenced twentieth-century history. This was particularly true of the first five. Each presided over a revolution which, though it would probably have occurred in one form or another in any case—since Russia, Germany, China and India were ripe for revolution in those times—would probably have taken quite other forms and directions had each of these individuals not been present at the critical moment. In a different way the same may be true of Roosevelt, Churchill and De Gaulle, since each of their countries faced a prodigious challenge in 1933, 1940 and 1958, respectively, and only they might have offered precisely the right saving response, without which their countries might not have been able to act effectively as significant powers in the ensuing period.

It is doubtful that one could justify a like claim about the successors of any of these men. Though they probably wished to expand Soviet power just as much as Stalin did, Khrushchev and those less remarkable *apparatchiks* who came after him necessarily took account of the realities of their times: the nuclear standoff and its potentiality for mutual destruction; the emergence of polycentrism inside the Communist "bloc," particularly in respect to China; and the recalcitrance both of the West and of most of the Third World to Marxist doctrine and Soviet pressure or infiltration. Others in their place would have had to reckon with the same realities, and given the relative uniformity of "personal histories" permitted in the Soviet Union (at least to persons rising to high office), would probably not have acted otherwise. The difference between Khrushchev on the one hand and Brezhnev and Kosygin on the other fairly well exhausts the range of realistic possibilities.

The spectrum of possible American Presidents is no doubt wider, as shown by the fact that since World War II both Adlai Stevenson and Barry Goldwater have been nominated for the Presidency by major parties. Still, none of those elected have been men of such overpowering genius that they can be said to have shaped their times. Rather, the times imposed constraints on them to which they have responded well or badly. Indeed, to one who has been able to observe U.S. Presidents and Secretaries of State closely over the past three decades, it is more remarkable how little, rather than how much, they seem able to resist or to guide the forces of history.

If one takes it as given that Stalin and his colleagues would behave as they did from 1945 to 1950, any American President accurately reflecting American character, American pride and American fears would have responded much as Truman did. It is probable that Thomas Dewey, had he been elected in 1944 or 1948, would have done the same. What Truman did not consider trying to do—what Roosevelt would almost certainly have at least attempted—would have been to exert more effort and offer more incentives to induce Stalin to behave differently, and at the same time to guide U.S. public opinion toward some semblance of "peaceful coexistence" rather than toward the grandiose global confrontation foreshadowed in the Truman Doctrine.

By 1953 the pattern of the Cold War was so firmly set on both sides that Stevenson could hardly have broken it, though he surely would have tried more boldly and more imaginatively to do so. I believe that, for instance, in the late fifties he would have responded with alacrity to the openings toward détente and to the more productive summit which Khrushchev seemed to offer.

As to Kennedy, Johnson and Nixon, each in his own way a man of goodwill, all were caught in the same web and each made some effort to break out of it. Kennedy's performance in his last year was impressive; had he lived longer he would no doubt have moved farther in the direction foreshadowed by his American University speech. Johnson, the least perceptive of the three, allowed himself to be almost wholly enmeshed in Vietnam; a wise man would have avoided this unnecessary entrapment. Nixon's sharp political instinct that the country and the world deeply desired to move from confrontation to negotiation was sound, and in his first year in office he did substantially that; in his second year he succumbed, as

Johnson had, to the will-o-the-wisp of victory in Vietnam and badly lost momentum; in the third and fourth years he returned more constructively toward negotiation, but was less able at so late a point to inspire the necessary confidence or demonstrate the necessary consistency.

In summary, it would seem that though they did what was necessary, with greater or less effectiveness, to preserve the national and Western security which Stalin had threatened, the five postwar U.S. Presidents, from Truman to Nixon, succumbed as easily as most of their fellow citizens to the stereotypes of their day and to the consuming fear of seeming soft or weak. With the exception of Kennedy in his last year, they all failed to demonstrate the deeper sagacity of a Lincoln, Wilson or Roosevelt which might have led them and their country much earlier out of the hazardous, costly and sterile competition of the Cold War.

The Evaluation
of Military Involvement
in Foreign Affairs

Since 1945 the military have played a role in the formulation and conduct of U.S. foreign affairs which, except in wartime, is wholly unprecedented in American history. During the past quarter-century practically no major decisions concerning foreign policy have been taken without the effective and intimate participation of the Secretary of Defense and the Joint Chiefs of Staff or their representatives.

Americans have often displayed a proclivity for electing military heroes to the Presidency—George Washington, Andrew Jackson, William Henry Harrison, Zachary Taylor, Ulysses Grant—but before 1945 neither these Presidents nor any other military leaders introduced in peacetime a military complexion or a preponderance of military considerations into American foreign policy. As recently as 1939 the U.S. armed forces numbered only 334,473, and the participation of their leaders, military or civilian, in governmental decision-making was limited to the organization and disposition of these modest forces.

The extraordinary escalation of the military role in in American government and politics after 1945 was a consequence of the deep fears aroused by Soviet imperialism and reflected a proximate consensus of U.S. opinion. It sprang from no calculated ambition or conspiracy of an officer corps hungry for power, nor from any abdication or incompetence of the civilians responsible for government. Neither did it arise from the inadvertent operation of Parkinson's Law, though that law did play a part in the process.

The military occupation of the center of the American political stage occurred because, between 1945 and 1950, both civilian and military leaders became passionately convinced that Communist expansion into Europe and Asia constituted a deadly threat to American security, a threat which could be deterred or resisted only by the mobilization of commensurate or superior military force. Whether or not it was based on an accurate assessment of Stalin's intentions and capabilities, this profound conviction was the fundamental determinant of U.S. and Western European foreign policy during the twenty years beginning in 1947.

It is worth noting, however, that the U.S.—far more than Europeans, oddly enough considering their respective histories—has chosen to exalt the role of the military in the elaboration and execution of the new policy. During these two decades, the Joint Chiefs of Staff, for example, had far more influence with both the President and the Congress than the politicians in Britain, France, Germany or Italy ever permitted their counterparts to enjoy. Until recently it has been sufficient for the Chiefs merely to present to the Congress their orders for more or newer weapons, no matter how costly, and be virtually certain that the legislative branch would docilely comply with almost no cavil or question.

The excessive participation of the U.S. military in foreign-policy-making began plausibly during World War II. Because of his naval experience and proclivities and his lack of respect for his own Secretary of State, Roosevelt relied for both strategic and political advice, when he sought it at all, primarily from his military chiefs. While the balance was somewhat redressed after the war through the tenure of such strong Secretaries of State as Byrnes, Marshall (himself a professional soldier), Acheson and Dulles, the close involvement of the military in foreign-policy-making continued unabated and almost unchallenged until very recently.

The immediate post-World War II arrangements, negotiated among the allies during the war, made inevitable a considerable involvement of the military in the conduct of foreign affairs because they provided for military government of the principal defeated enemies, Germany and Japan; for the division of Germany, Austria and Korea into military zones of occupation; for the establishment of multipartite control commissions, all staffed primarily by military men, in Germany, Austria, Italy, Japan, Korea, Hungary, Rumania and Bulgaria. Originally it had been supposed that these arrangements would be of brief duration. At Yalta Roosevelt declared that American troops must be out of Europe within two years of the end of the war, and indeed the U.S. Army was so rapidly demobilized that it declined from a peak of 8.3 million on V-E Day to 1.9 million a year later. It was intended, moreover, that military governments would be rapidly superseded by indigenous civilian governments in all of the occupied countries.

However, most of these intentions were swept away by the onset of the Cold War. The events of the years 1945 to 1950 persuaded the American leadership that the common ambition of Stalin and Mao was world domination, and they responded with the creation of NATO and SEATO, the rearmament of Germany, a massive military riposte in Korea, deployment of American fleets in the Mediterranean and the Taiwan straits, and aid programs supervised by substantial U.S. military groups in many parts of the world. These circumstances convinced our civilian leadership that foreign policy and national security were inextricably intertwined, and hence that the entrenchment of military officers at the heart of the foreign policy decision-making process in Washington was proper and necessary.

As early as 1947 the involvement of the military in this process was institutionalized when President Truman requested and Congress adopted the National Security Act, which, *inter alia,* created the National Security Council. The duties of this body were described in the Act as "(1) to assess and appraise the objectives, commitments and risks of the United States in relation to our actual and political military power, in the interest of national security, for the purpose of making recommendations to the President in connection therewith; and (2) to consider policies on matters of common interest to the departments and agencies of the government concerned with the national security, and to make recommendations to the President in connection therewith."

This second "duty" was the catchall which ultimately came to embrace almost all of our foreign policy. The original membership of the Council included the Secretary of Defense and the official now known as the Director of the Office of Emergency Preparedness, but no military officers. However, the Chairman of the Joint Chiefs of Staff and the Director of the Central Intelligence Agency (an institution also created by the National Security Act of 1947) have normally been considered as ex-officio members and have regularly sat with the Council.

Underneath the Council there grew up a vast apparatus

—originally for the most part in the State and Defense Departments, but in recent years also in the White House itself—of interdepartmental committees, groups and task forces charged in fact, if not always in name, with reviewing, recommending or deciding policies and action over most of the area of foreign affairs. Military and civilian representatives of the Defense Department, often men of great ability and strength of character, have participated in all these committees and have from time to time exercised predominant influence over them. As evidence of their decisive weight—much greater, for example, than that of their counterparts in any of our European allies—one only has to recall the names of James Forrestal, General Alfred Gruenther, General Lucius Clay, General Lauris Norstad, Admiral Arthur Radford, General Curtis LeMay, General Maxwell Taylor, Robert McNamara and General William Westmoreland.

On the basis of the meager information on the subject which trickles through the Iron Curtain, it has always been impossible to determine the extent to which generals and admirals are similarly involved in policy-making and resource allocation in the Soviet Union. On the one hand, the Communist Party and its leaders have always been incontestably supreme, to such a degree that Stalin was able without the slightest difficulty to liquidate most of the high command of the Red Army in the late 1930's, and Khrushchev was as easily able to purge Zhukov in 1957 just after he had availed himself of the marshal's aid to oust his own political rivals. On the other hand, presumably because Soviet leaders like Western ones, believed their national security to be critically threatened, the Soviet military have apparently been increasingly influential in national councils since Stalin's death. No doubt they supported, if they did not actually assist in, Khrushchev's removal, since presumably he had in their view failed to allocate sufficient resources to the armed forces and had presided over their humiliating reversal in Cuba.

Such evidence as is available suggests that the Russian military are particularly close to Brezhnev.

About 10 percent of the Soviet gross national product is devoted to "defense," and apparently the admirals and generals have obtained during the past seven or eight years almost everything they have requested in the way of armaments, since the buildup, particularly in strategic weapons and naval ships, has been as extravagant as even the most gluttonous military stomach could desire.

What role they play in foreign policy decision-making—on Germany, Czechoslovakia, the Middle East, China and Vietnam—is much more difficult to estimate. They lack the valuable recourse of their American counterparts to sympathetic elements in the Congress and public opinion, but they form a part of a military-industrial complex which, because of the nature of the Communist system, is even more integrated into government than ours is. Moreover, when they are deployed abroad, they probably enjoy some of the same de facto autonomy that our military do. I well remember, when I reproached a representative of the Soviet Foreign Ministry in September 1970 for the movement of Soviet-manned missiles up to the Suez Canal in violation of the recent standstill agreement, he responded somewhat shame-facedly, "Oh, that was another ministry."

Hence, we are probably justified in believing that the inflation of the military role in foreign affairs is almost equally present in the Soviet Union. Indeed, one might say that the role of each reflects, reciprocates and feeds on the other; that the American general or admiral exists by virtue of the existence of an equivalent Soviet general or admiral; that each is in fact the shadow of the other and could not survive the disappearance of his counterpart. It is fascinating how in private conversations men in each military establishment refer to men in the other in respectful, almost comradely terms.

In regard to the other Communist great power, it is

perhaps also worth noting that the Chinese People's Army, in contrast to the traditionally undistinguished role of the military in Chinese life, has been close to the center of power from its inception. This is no doubt a consequence of twenty years of civil war, of the war against Japan and of the Korean War. Though before, during and after the Cultural Revolution many of their leaders, including Lin Piao, were purged, more recently the concurrent weakening of the party apparatus has resulted in the assumption by the military of wide political and economic responsibilities throughout China. It can be presumed that military influence in the formulation and conduct of foreign policy is also considerable, though fortunately it would appear that the objectives of the Chinese military are, at least for the present, modest and defensive.

That this need not necessarily have been the case is suggested by a brief encounter I had in 1946 when I was chargé d'affaires in Bangkok. The Thais, their country having been occupied by the Japanese, had had no contact with the Chinese during the war, but it now became expedient to reestablish relations, particularly since they could not enter the United Nations without Chinese acquiescence in the Security Council vote. At Thai invitation, therefore, the Chinese Nationalist government dispatched a special emissary to negotiate the establishment of diplomatic relations. For reasons not entirely clear to me, the Chinese sent for this purpose not a diplomat but a bluff and doughty general. When I paid a call on this representative of one of our closest allies, he proved to be far less interested in discussing relations with Thailand than in explaining to me, over two or three glasses of whiskey, how easy it would be for the United States and China together—we with our marvelous weaponry and they with their limitless manpower—to conquer the world. He was eager to pursue this subject in detail and was obviously disappointed when I showed no interest. I have often wondered what has happened to him.

A six-year war involving all the major powers and most of the lesser ones, followed almost immediately by a martial confrontation between two groups of powers —each convinced the other was bent on its destruction—therefore elevated the military, certainly in the United States and perhaps also in the Soviet Union, to a central position in the foreign policy decision-making apparatus of their countries. Unfortunately this occurred at precisely the moment when a monstrous revolution in weaponry disrupted the relative stability of prewar weapons systems and raised international competition in arms to levels that were more hazardous, more costly and more unpredictable than ever before.

Developed within a short space of time were, first, atomic and then hydrogen explosives, long-range and supersonic aircraft for their delivery, tactical and intercontinental missiles, both land-based and sea-based, with nuclear and, later, multiple reentry warheads, antiballistic missile defenses, atomic-powered surface ships and submarines, and countless variations and refinements on each of these inventions. Military men have always justified multiplying armaments, old and new, on the ground that the enemy was already doing so and that it would be dangerous to fall behind. But during this twenty-five-year period they were able to argue, rightly or wrongly, that the enemy's superiority in one or more of the new weapons systems could suddenly result not merely in defeat but in annihilation, not only of their armies and navies, but of much of the civil population.

Hence there grew up, and still continues, an arms race of fantastic scale, which seems to feed on its own technological momentum and to be almost uncontrollable by human will. Each participant spends vast sums on research and development in a desperate effort to surpass or forestall developments by the other side, but such is the unity of science and the involuntary symbiosis between "progress" on one side and that on the other that whatever one side discovers the other soon repeats, and neither ever moves far enough ahead to feel confident or secure.

This compulsive international competition is further stimulated, at least on the American side, by two contributing factors. The first is a subtle combination of interservice rivalry and collusion. Historically, armed forces have long been administratively divided into armies and navies, and since World War I, air forces have also been widely established as a separate service. It is doubtful that under present circumstances this tripartite division serves any useful national purpose, except insofar as interservice competition contributes marginally to alertness, diligence and morale. On the other hand, the fact that three separate and equal services exist, each represented at the Chiefs of Staff and sub-Cabinet level, each participating in the process of weapons development and budget preparation, means that each will demand and obtain a substantial share in defense responsibilities and defense funds. Moreover, each will seek to increase as much as possible the funds, weapons and manpower available to it—first, because the more it has the more confident it is of successfully performing its mission "if the balloon goes up"; second, because power and prestige obviously accrue to a service and its officer corps which is playing an expanding part in war and peace. Finally, since all three services have a common interest in getting as large a pie as possible to divide among them, they will usually close ranks before the Congress, and even before the President, in insisting jointly that the whole range of the demands of each service is essential to national security.

The consequence of this all-too-human process is all too obvious: redundancy on a colossal scale. The most glaring example is in the strategic field, where one finds three distinct systems for the transcontinental delivery of nuclear weapons: long-range aircraft, intercontinental land-based missiles and sea-based missiles. Objectively speaking, it is not at all clear that the last, which are far and away the least vulnerable and which do not invite preemptive or retaliatory attack on the United States, would not alone be quite sufficient. It could be cogently argued that the first two exist in large part for the benefit of the Air Force rather than of an essential national interest. In fact, it is also not at all clear that the creation of a third separate service—the Air Force—was either necessary or desirable. Experience with aerial bombing in World War II, Korea and Vietnam suggests not only that its independent accomplishments are far less than its proponents have claimed, not only that it is the most callous and barbaric form of modern warfare, but also that it can best serve realistic military purposes by being used as a closely integrated supplement to ground and naval action.

Lest I should be accused of undue bias in favor of the Navy, let me add that I am far from convinced that the national interest is served by our having substantial task forces of surface ships (primarily aircraft carriers and their escorts) cruising about the seven seas. Aside from a contribution to the bombing of Vietnam, their primary tangible accomplishment during recent years seems to have been to convince the Soviet admirals and government of the vital necessity of matching them, of attaining "parity" in the naval as in the missile arm. The result is that a new arena of costly military competition between the United States and the USSR is opening up, and admirals on both sides are predicting imminent doom to their respective governments if their escalating demands for more ships are not satisfied. If they should be, and if rival U.S. and Soviet task forces roam about the Mediterranean, Persian Gulf, Indian Ocean and Western Pacific more and more frequently, the temptation to use them in ways which are equally hazardous to each other and to innocent bystanders will not be easily resisted. The more gunboats there are, the more appealing and common will be the occasions for the exercise of gunboat diplomacy.

I have never personally been persuaded that such exercises are particularly rewarding. One with which I had some experience was the celebrated landing in Lebanon in 1958. This was carried out with great efficiency and restraint but was entirely unnecessary. The Lebanese civil war had broken out primarily because President Camille Chamoun, with the help of our CIA, had so outrageously manipulated the last election that his opponents refused to accept its results. The U.S. government felt obliged to intervene because it had unwisely given a "guarantee" to Chamoun under the misplaced Eisenhower Doctrine. The immediate consequence of our intervention was to end the civil war but to place the opponents of Chamoun firmly in office, where they remained for many years.

The second domestic factor contributing to international competition in arms is, of course, that well-advertised if ill-defined behemoth: the military-industrial complex. Enough has been said about it so that it need not be discussed here except to note that whatever its exact dimensions and character may be, it certainly contributes substantially to the incessant multiplication of weapons; that it creates a strong vested interest in the arms race on the part of powerful industries, their employees, stockholders, and those who represent them in Congress; and that it therefore contributes considerably to the excessive influence of military men and military considerations in the conduct of foreign affairs.

However, two parenthetical comments might be made in this connection. First, it is not widely known that General Eisenhower was not the only celebrated military leader who warned against the military-industrial complex. In addressing a joint session of the Michigan State Legislature on May 15, 1952, General Douglas MacArthur stated: "Indeed, it is part of the general pattern of misguided policy that our country is now geared to an arms economy which was bred in an artificially induced psychosis of war hysteria and nurtured upon an incessant propaganda of fear. While such an economy may produce a sense of seeming prosperity for the moment, it rests on an illusionary foundation of complete unreliability and renders among our political leaders almost a greater fear of peace than is their fear of war."

Secondly, if the vast accumulation of arms throughout the world leads to general war, it will be the greatest catastrophe in human history; if it does not, it will be the greatest boondoggle in human history.

It will be useful at this point to analyze more rigorously the military and political assumptions on which this exorbitant military buildup is based and through which it is justified by both its military and civilian proponents. The two most fundamental and most vulnerable of these assumptions are, first, the usual postulation of "worst case" in regard to the capabilities of the adversary; and second, the simplistic confusion between his capabilities and his intentions.

As to the first, in estimating the manpower and arsenals of the other side and judging their capabilities, each side "plays it safe" by assuming the most extravagant end of the conceivable spectrum to be the correct one. The most alarming intelligence reports are accepted as probably correct; the adversary is presumed to be going all out on any system of which there is any evidence of development and deployment; each of his systems, no matter how untested under conditions of real war, is assumed to work perfectly in combat. On the basis of these extremely flattering estimates of the adversary's capabilities—usually accompanied by a gloomy assessment of one's own—the military services repeatedly claim that they will be disastrously defeated come Doomsday if not given sufficient resources to match all the inordinate assumptions they have made about the weaponry of the other side. The result is, for example, that one side imagines a vast "missile gap" to its detriment, builds massively to fill that gap, and in so doing creates a *real* missile gap against the other side—which thereupon builds even more massively to overcome the gap and to create a new one to its advantage. And so it goes.

The second familiar false assumption in the bipolar adversary relationship is that the adversary's intentions are consonant with his capabilities, though of course one's own are not, since ours are always peaceful and defensive. For example, if the Soviet Union maintains huge and well-equipped ground forces allegedly superior in capabilities to the NATO forces opposed to them, it follows that the Soviets will eventually seize a favorable opportunity to march to the English Channel. Or if the Soviets are expanding massively their offensive missile system on land and sea, this means not only that they will soon achieve decisive superiority if the United States does not immediately match their hypothetical goals, but that they will use their superiority once achieved to exercise nuclear blackmail—to demand that we get out of the Mediterranean or Europe or, in the most extravagant example, install an American Quisling in the White House.

Since this postulated threat of nuclear blackmail is the theoretical foundation for most of the competition in strategic arms, and for much of the military involvement in the conduct of foreign affairs, it is worthwhile to examine in some detail and with sober skepticism the kind of scenario presented by the military and civilian proponents of this popular fantasy. If an ultimatum of this sort came over the "hot line" from the Kremlin, I suspect that any American President would react in one of two ways. If he took the threat seriously and thought the choice was inescapably between surrender or annihilation, he would immediately launch a first strike himself in order to destroy as much of the Soviet arsenal as possible. Since this American reaction would be clearly foreseeable, it seems unlikely that any Soviet leader would pose a threat in such a form and incur so grave a risk of a first strike against his country.

However, in the belief that it was a crude sort of bluff, the more probable response of an American President to such blackmail would be simply to answer by total rejection. Unless the Russians were thereupon prepared to launch a first strike, they would have to swallow the rejection, and thus appear to the world both criminal and weak. Yet, is it conceivable that they *would* launch a first strike, given the fact that U.S. seaborne missiles will long be invulnerable and that no one can be certain, until they are tried in wartime, of the efficacy of any ABM systems either they or we have? Undoubtedly the Soviets would have foreseen the dilemma into which crude nuclear blackmail of this kind would be likely to draw them, and hence would hardly undertake it in the first place, even if they *had* arrived at the superiority which the "worst case" supposes.

However, there is another, slightly more sophisticated scenario which the cold warriors of the "worst case" also unroll. In this one the Soviets take advantage of superiority in conventional forces and arms to threaten or impose demands on the West which can be successfully resisted only by resort to nuclear arms—to which, however, under the "worst case" assumption, the West would not dare resort because of its strategic inferiority. Therefore it would supposedly have to surrender what was demanded. Berlin has been the favorite presumed target for this sort of blackmail, since it is surrounded by Soviet forces, but as Soviet naval power grows in the Mediterranean we shall no doubt be hearing that Israel or the Persian Gulf or the Sixth Fleet itself constitutes another such hostage.

The elements of unreality in these scenarios are basically the same as in the previously cited example of crude nuclear blackmail, and essentially the response of an

American President would be similar. Mere threats would simply be rejected out of hand. If the Soviets chose actually to use conventional military force around Berlin, in the Mediterranean or elsewhere, and this force proved to be greater than could be coped with by conventional response, tactical nuclear weapons would be employed. The Soviets are aware that employment of such weapons is programmed under these circumstances. It is also a part of their own military doctrine that once any sort of nuclear weapon has been used, every sort is likely to be used. They have no way of knowing how this escalation would take place, who would act first at each stage and who would suffer most. What they *do* know is that the rhythm, once started, could not be controlled by anyone, and that it could easily develop in such a way as to lead to the destruction of much of the Soviet Union. /57261/

Therefore, even if one assumes Soviet superiority in conventional forces and arms at certain points, and one also assumes the "worst case" of Soviet strategic nuclear superiority, the Kremlin would be confronted by the same insoluble dilemmas and enormous hazards if it tried to apply nuclear blackmail. The scenarios imagined for their doing so are the sheerest fantasy and take no account of the consistent characteristics of Soviet foreign policy over the past half century. If Soviet leaders were cornered and saw no other means of survival as a great power, they might engage in one of the reckless gambles which these scenarios suppose. Under present and foreseeable circumstances, however, we cannot imagine their risking their own power and all they have built over fifty years for spectacular gains which they do not need, and which, according to their own dogmas, will eventually fall into their laps in any case.

What conclusion should we draw if skepticism about the apocalyptic consequences of the "worst case" is correct? Not a very new or startling one, and certainly not that we can afford to disarm unilaterally. Rather, only that many of our military strategists and professional Cassandras are living in a nightmare world of their own devising. Neither side in the stupid nuclear arms race needs to match the other in every particular, or even in most particulars. As long as each has and can keep an invulnerable core of strategic weapons able to wreak enormous devastation on the adversary who lacks any corresponding defense on which he could rely with certainty, that is enough; that is "sufficiency." All the rest is frills and luxuries, unessential to real security, capable only of aggravating the fears and increasing the armaments of the adversary, valuable only for supporting competing armed services in the boundless extravagance to which we have allowed them to become accustomed. As long as an invulnerable deterrent core is there, whatever other strategic superiority one side or the other may have, no leader in his right mind would risk resorting seriously to nuclear blackmail. If he did he would be checkmated and humiliated, would immeasurably strengthen the cohesion of the opposing alliance and would redouble its arms production and deployment.

The heart of the matter was succinctly put by U Thant, the Secretary General of the United Nations, in the introduction to his *Annual Report* for 1968: "The only reason which could induce either the Soviet Union and its allies, or the Western Powers, to attack the other would be a pervading fear by one side of a preemptive strike by the other. This fear is fed by, and grows proportionately with, the increase of the offensive military power of the two superstates. It is, clearly, the build-up of excessive military power beyond any reasonable demands of defense which has become the most ominous threat to world peace."

In other words, whatever the purpose of the armament of the superpowers may be thought or claimed to be, it is in fact no longer a shield protecting their peoples but itself the most serious threat to the survival of these peoples.

Furthermore, so paradoxical has the situation become that, whenever American members of Congress vote money for arms, they should be aware that in so doing they are at the same time voting for the Soviet arms which will be built to match or outdo those on the American side. When Congress votes funds for a submarine, it votes not for one but for two, an American and a Soviet.

One could linger on the zigzags of strategic doctrine—from "containment" to "massive retaliation" to "deterrence" and "graduated response"—and on the Byzantine political gambits, foreign and domestic, which flow from these military postures, but I think the point has been sufficiently made. In order to complete the case in regard to military involvement in foreign affairs, however, it is necessary to deal briefly with participation in military alliances, and with military deployments and operations overseas.

Military alliances are indispensable under certain circumstances, but like all institutions as they age they tend to fossilize and to resist adaptation to changing circumstances. The North Atlantic Treaty Organization filled a vital need when it was established—that of quickly and unmistakably diminishing the temptation to Stalin to expand further into the soft center of postwar Europe. An elaborate military structure and a complementary political apparatus for continuous consultation were set up with this end in view. This structure and apparatus were remarkably successful in uniting North American and West European governments and peoples in this cause, and in containing Soviet expansion at the point it had reached in 1948. It was a momentous accomplishment, but did entail some unfortunate side effects which are pertinent to my argument.

First, the character of the alliance tended to place our relations with many of our closest friends, the West Europeans, in a predominantly military context, and to position ministers of defense, generals and admirals at the heart not only of the NATO military structure but of the complementary apparatus for political consultation. As a result, for more than twenty years the predominant vehicle for conducting our relations with the British, French, Germans, Italians and others has had a strong military cast and has emphasized military aims, military dangers, military cooperation, military budgets and weapons systems. Up to a point, this was necessary, but it was probably carried farther than was required. It certainly contributed substantially to the tendency in Washington to involve the military closely in a decision-making process which was often, strictly speaking, more concerned with political than with military affairs.

A second unfortunate effect of the creation of the elaborate NATO structure was the degree to which it took on a persistent life of its own and the consequent difficulty of adapting it to changing circumstances. On the one hand, as the years passed, the Western European countries recovered their economic and political strength, became much less vulnerable to Soviet pressure, and could have contributed a much larger share to the military and financial support of the alliance. That they were politically unwilling to do so, and at the same time psychologically reluctant to have the American military presence reduced, led to constant transatlantic bickering, which at times seemed to dominate relations between the United States and its closest allies.

By the beginning of the 1970's the Sino-Soviet schism had reduced Soviet ability and willingness to risk adventures in the West and Willy Brandt's rapprochement with Moscow and Warsaw had induced a marked feeling of détente in Europe. There was a general desire to adjust the structured and cumbersome apparatus of NATO to the new realities, but no one was quite sure how to go about it. Few wanted to risk dismantling it, for there was no certainty as to what the Kremlin leadership, living in so strange and unventilated a world as theirs, might decide to do a year or five years hence. Perhaps the Russians would misinterpret détente for appeasement and think they could gradually mold or squeeze the whole of Europe into the posture of Finland or even Czechoslovakia. Obviously any overt effort to do so would immediately restore and revitalize the Western alliance as nothing else could. There was much talk of a European security conference and of "mutual balanced force reductions," but would it prove to be more than talk? In the meantime the problem was to keep the machinery of NATO from breaking down or rusting while at the same time diminishing, to the degree the Soviet posture would permit, the militarization of Europe, East and West, to conform to a new era with new goals, new problems and new imperatives.

If NATO still has a significant role to play, the same cannot be said of the Southeast Asia Treaty Organization, which was never more than a transparent cover for U.S. military support of a few Southeast Asian nations, most of which were less immediately threatened by external attack than by their own failure to reform their archaic political and economic structures. Yet, in imitation of the NATO pattern, a similar elaborate military and political apparatus was created for SEATO, and from 1954 on, the problems of the treaty area were viewed and dealt with primarily from a military perspective. This may be one of the underlying reasons why the United States slipped so easily into massive military involvement in Vietnam.

A third unfortunate side effect of grand military alliances has been the necessity they imposed—an unavoidable necessity, at least at the outset—of stationing large bodies of U.S. military forces far from the United States, and of scattering smaller complementary military bases in a large number of countries. This requirement, real in some cases, fanciful in others, creates serious problems in the conduct of our foreign relations, more with our friends than with our adversaries. In almost every case the numbers were considerably larger than they need have been, the special privileges accorded the Americans were unnecessarily great, and the high visibility of troops and privileges often became, particularly as the external threat diminished, an affront to the indigenous population. Our relations with Turkey and the Philippines, for example, have been severely affected by popular resentment on this score. The question of sharing the financial burden of supporting such troops has been for a long time a source of acrimonious debate with Germany and Spain.

For some time, bases in so-called nonaligned countries, such as Morocco and Libya, poisoned our relations with these countries and their neighbors. When the Moroccans during my tenure as ambassador demanded the removal of our air bases installed there under the French, the U.S. military protested in the most categorical terms—I recall particularly the language used by General LeMay—that loss of the bases would do the gravest harm to American security. After they had been given up nevertheless, the loss was apparently hardly felt at all. Conversely, military insistence on the indispensability of bases in the Azores prevailed with three U.S. administrations, continues to bind us to Portugal's antiquated colonial policy and still troubles our relations with forty African nations. Arguments with Japan about Okinawa and nuclear weapons on Japanese soil have been a continuous source of recrimination and are far from wholly resolved.

All of these global deployments and presences have inevitably been a further occasion for involving the military in the conduct of foreign affairs, and often for casting our foreign policy in preponderantly military terms. The Pentagon and the Joint Chiefs must be consulted about almost all matters affecting relations with countries where these deployments and bases exist. Their presence becomes a useful source of blackmail against the United States by the host country, and, as in the case of the Azores, preservation of the bases is often given priority over important political considerations affecting either the host country or others. For example, the leverage over the United States presently enjoyed by the military governments of Spain and Greece because of our bases there decisively affects our political posture toward those governments. Our military presence and posture in the Canal Zone has caused constant trouble with Panama.

The list could be further prolonged, but the point is clear. Some of these deployments and bases are still necessary; many are not. All are enormously complicating factors in the conduct of foreign affairs, and all involve the military establishment in that conduct in a way that easily distorts policy.

Finally, our vast military-aid programs should be mentioned: aid to our NATO and SEATO allies, aid to Ethiopia, the Congo and many other nations of Africa, and most of all, aid to our fighting allies in two wars—South Korea, South Vietnam, Laos and Cambodia. In each case there had to be stationed in the recipient country a Military Assistance Advisory Group to train the local forces in the use of the arms received, and to make sure they were used for the purpose intended. In countries where the programs were substantial or where the local military establishment was unsophisticated, these MAAG's became very large indeed. They sometimes came not only to dominate the military policy of the country in question, but if the local military played a political role, to influence the foreign and domestic politics of the host country.

Normally, the generals or colonels in command of these MAAG's, as well as the army, navy and air attachés, were members of the "country team," which, under the chairmanship of the U.S. ambassador, sought to coordinate policy and action of the numerous and powerful U.S. agencies operating in the host country. The resources available to the MAAG chief, however, were well in excess of those available to the ambassador himself. If the ambassador was firm and competent and the MAAG chief had a properly restricted conception of *his* functions, reasonable coordination occurred. If one or both of these conditions did not obtain, the MAAG chief sometimes came to be more instrumental in conveying U.S.—or occasionally his own—policies to the host government than did the ambassador himself.

Another consequence of the power and proliferation of MAAG's, particularly in countries where there was armed subversion or insurgency, was that as the aid programs grew larger to meet the challenge, the MAAG's likewise grew to vast proportions. Moreover, they tended, not unnaturally, to acquire a vested interest in the success of their clients, to extend their "advisory" function closer and closer to the field of operations or of battle, and in some cases, with or without prior authorization, to become themselves directly involved in combat. This became especially prevalent after Washington at the outset of the Kennedy Administration became intoxicated with the concept of "counterinsurgency" and began to nourish the odd illusion (to which I referred earlier) that American officers trained at Fort Bragg could train Vietnamese to fight and beat Viet Cong in Asian jungles. To be sure, this shift in emphasis was something of an improvement over the earlier error, indulged in after 1954, of training Vietnamese to fight a Korean-style war, which of course never came. Nevertheless, the counterinsurgency fad had the effect of involving more and more Americans in combat operations, and hence of leading imperceptibly into the massive involvement of 1965 and thereafter.

The sum of all these developments during the twenty-five years after World War II was not only to create in the Pentagon the most gigantic and affluent military bureaucracy the world has ever seen, but to distribute throughout the foreign-affairs apparatus—in Washington and over-seas—representatives of this bureaucracy authorized to participate, in varying degrees, in the formulation and conduct of foreign policy. These representatives are honorable and intelligent men highly trained in their profession. Their first loyalty, however, is naturally to their conception of the national interest, and to the service in which they are making their career. They perceive the components of foreign affairs through the prism of what they believe to be overriding military necessities. Relations with the Soviet Union, for example, must for them be governed by the necessity, at whatever internal or external cost, of maintaining a panoply of weapons—ever widening as technology spawns its latest nightmares—able to repel any conceivable form of Soviet attack against the United States or any of its allies. Relations with those allies must be governed by the necessity of persuading or obliging them to make the greatest extractable contribution to the common military effort, and of dissuading them from making any dangerous accommodations with the adversary. Relations with neutral or nonaligned states must be governed by the necessity of ensuring that they are not dominated or manipulated by the adversary and of taking whatever steps, no matter how provocative or inimical, are necessary to prevent such domination or manipulation.

It is not at all clear that men so motivated and so trained, even though most honorably, should be as deeply involved in the conduct of foreign affairs as they are. There is even some doubt whether, in a world so precariously poised on an atom, they are psychologically best fitted to define and judge national security in its broadest sense. Almost a century ago a sagacious British Prime Minister, Lord Salisbury, said to a colleague: "You listen too much to the soldiers . . . You should never trust the experts. If you believe the doctors, nothing is wholesome; if you believe the theologians, nothing is innocent; if you believe the soldiers, nothing is safe." In his account of the Cuban missile crisis, Robert Kennedy comments at one point: "One member of the Joint Chiefs of Staff argued that we could use nuclear weapons, on the basis that our adversaries would use theirs against us in an attack. I thought, as I listened, of the many times that I had heard the military take positions which, if wrong, had the advantage that no one would be around at the end to know."*

The fact is that thanks to the new wonder weapons developed and deployed since 1945, the United States has never before been both so heavily armed and so insecure. Despite our relatively modest forces and armaments in 1941, the most extreme damage to our national security which it was feasible for an enemy to inflict was that effected by the Japanese at Pearl Harbor. Despite our enormous arsenals, in 1972 there is nothing—*nothing*—we could do to prevent the extermination of about half our population in a matter of days or hours if general war occurred. The same is true of the Soviet Union.

This truly appalling situation is not the fault of military men, but it is also *not* a situation which can be corrected by military means. Following the advice of their military commanders, both the United States and the Soviet Union have been endeavoring, for the past quarter century, to reinforce their national security and reestablish some measure of invulnerability by developing and deploying new, more sophisticated and more destructive weapons systems. The result of all these ingenious and costly dispositions is that we are more nakedly and hideously vulnerable than ever. There is no reason whatsoever to believe that following the same course for another twenty-five years—if we last that long—would make us in the slightest degree more secure.

Reasonable men and women will not tolerate such folly indefinitely. As Henry Kissinger wrote shortly before he took over as National Security Adviser: "It will become more and more difficult to demonstrate that *anything* is worse than the elimination of over half a society in a

*Robert Kennedy, *Thirteen Days* (New York: W. W. Norton, 1969).

matter of days."* The way out of the mess we have got ourselves into is neither clear nor easy, but it is certainly not a military way. I shall have more to say about what it might be later on. The point I wish to make here is that, since the traditional military mind seems ill-adapted to comprehending the new character and requirements of national security under modern conditions, it is not likely that men trained in that tradition can contribute to the formulation of new foreign policies better suited to that end. Yet the swift determination and execution of such policies is clearly essential to the survival of civilization.

It would therefore be expedient and sensible, as one step in that direction, if the role of the military in the formulation and conduct of foreign policy was limited, as it is in most other countries and traditionally has been in this one, to appraisals of what is or is not militarily feasible or wise, and to the execution of policies laid down by civilians on the basis of much more comprehensive considerations. Such a reversal of a thirty-year trend, such a revamping and modernization of established machinery and practices, would of course be painful and slow, but until it is carried out there is little prospect of a wiser and more far-sighted conduct of foreign affairs.

The Identity Crisis of Nationalism:
Competition in, about and among
Less Developed Countries

Since World War II nearly seventy former colonies have gained or regained independence. Adding twenty Latin American countries, plus a few others which emerged from colonialism between the two world wars, brings the

---

*Henry Kissinger, *American Foreign Policy: Three Essays* (New York: W. W. Norton, 1969).

total to about ninety-five which fall within the broad category of less developed or developing nations. Even if one excludes China from this number (though it is certainly underdeveloped), their aggregate population is about two billion, or more than half that of the world. Moreover, these states make up more than 70 percent of the membership of the United Nations.

Naturally, the emergence in so short a time of this large number of new states, each confronting independently the desperate problems of underdevelopment, has enormously complicated the conduct of foreign affairs in the late-twentieth century. No matter how unjust and oppressive nineteenth-century imperialism was, it had at least the virtue of simplicity, of centering in a relatively few capitals responsibility for most foreign affairs. In addition, except for Washington and Tokyo, these responsible capitals, were all located in one geographic area, Europe.

This was an extremely artificial and unstable arrangement which came about only because the Europeans had been first to master certain critical technologies. As soon as these technologies were sufficiently disseminated, the demand for independence became imperative and the cost of resisting it became too great for most colonial powers to bear. The reason why the Russian Empire survived all the others was partly that the subject territories were contiguous and easily accessible to the imperial state, and partly that the subject peoples were only marginally exposed to libertarian doctrine, either before or after the Communist revolution.

One of the main causes of World War I was rivalry among the great powers over such underdeveloped areas as the Balkans, Africa and China, in which they claimed political or economic interests. While great-power interests outside their own territories are now much more effectively resisted by what one might now call "object" rather than "subject" peoples, nevertheless those interests have become geographically more far-flung in the late twentieth century, since every great power is now able to claim at least some interest in most of the ninety-five independent developing countries. Of course, the powers that are sufficiently "great" to make such extensive claims are limited: the United States, the Soviet Union, the European Common Market complex, Japan and potentially China. It goes without saying that the Cold War has greatly aggravated and polarized these great-power rivalries in the Third World.

Before discussing further the behavior of great powers in and about developing countries, it may be useful to examine briefly the political, economic and social climate in these countries, and the reasons why they are at this stage inevitably so disturbed and vulnerable. As Lester Pearson said in his celebrated report of 1969 to the International Bank: "Development is not a guarantee of political stability or an antidote to violence. Change is, itself, intrinsically disruptive." Never have most of the countries in question been subjected in so short a time to change so disruptive and so devastating. And the process has just begun.

Since the white peoples of Europe and North America, who developed economically and "modernized" politically during the nineteenth and first half of the twentieth centuries, often smugly assume that they were able to do so with such remarkable success because of innate and distinctive qualities either of mind or civilization, it is useful to point out the peculiar advantages they enjoyed. First, most of them inhabited nation-states firmly established, centrally governed, and endowed with trained elites for centuries before the Industrial Revolution took place. (Even so, their histories between, say, 1775 and 1950 hardly offer convincing evidence of innate talent for harmonious and rational development.) Second, these countries made the transition into modern industrial society before the revolution in medicine, and while population growth was still deliberate and manageable. Third, the same deliberate pace characterized the mass movement from rural to urban areas which provided the work force for industrial society. Finally, the stretching out of these changes over many decades, together with the much more elementary character of public information before the invention of radio and television, softened their immediate impact on the mass of the population affected, allowed time for assimilation of them to take place almost imperceptibly, and muted and slowed expectations of the benefits to the common man which the revolution in production could bring.

The situation is vastly different in those nations which became independent after World War II or, even if independent long before that time, had not earlier directly experienced the Industrial Revolution and its consequences. Many of the new countries have only an incomplete sense of national identity. They were created through the accidents and rivalries of imperialism which sometimes flung together ill-assorted and hostile ethnic groups, and sometimes separated homogeneous groups. Their boundaries often make neither political nor economic sense; they are sometimes too large to be politically cohesive and often too small to be economically viable. Some have a glorious history but one too ancient to be currently relevant; others search vainly for any historical identity at all. Some are more or less homogeneous culturally and sociologically; others contain half a dozen separate cultures, of which some may be half modern and others mostly primitive and archaic. The majority of them may be said to be nations in search of a soul.

Secondly, thanks to the medical revolution of the last half century, many of these new nations have a population growing so rapidly that the benefits of economic development, even when significant in the aggregate, are for most individuals almost imperceptible. Death control was enormously successful before birth control had any impact at all; indeed, in many countries the latter is for a variety of reasons fiercely resisted. Yet if current rates of population growth continue, it is hard to see how many less developed countries can survive.

Thirdly, a vastly disproportionate part of this new population is flowing into great urban agglomerations. As the need for more food to feed more people grows geometrically, age-old systems of subsistence farming on small plots must give way to large-scale production with new methods and new machines. The result is the rapid displacement of millions from the land who then stream beggared into the cities. These urban areas, however, are totally unable to cope with this colossal immigration. Lacking either capital or effective producing power to permit quick and substantial industrial growth, they can offer employment for only a fraction of the immigrants. The tax revenues of the cities, or even of their national governments, are wholly insufficient to provide even a minimum of municipal services—sewage, disposal, housing, electricity, streets and transportation, health care and hospitals, schools and recreation. The inevitable consequence is the transformation of many of the already poverty-stricken cities of Asia, Latin America and Africa into huge, indecent, festering and hopeless human antheaps, of which Calcutta is the archetype. Yet the incoming flood continues unabated, and there is no real prospect that in the near future it can be either coped with or checked.

Fourthly, for the most part the people of these countries lack any experience in governing themselves. More important, they either lack an elite with experience in this essential business, or the existing elite is indifferent to public welfare because of its tradition of family self-interest. Both old and new elites are often grossly inefficient or shockingly corrupt, and this is why in so many developing countries (including many long independent like the Latin Americas) the military officers corps, constituting either the only relatively effective or the only

relatively disinterested elite, has taken over the government. Unfortunately, the temptations of power have often
proved too much for them to resist, and the result is
military dictatorship.

Fifthly, the prospects of overcoming these political
handicaps in the near future are severely limited in most
of these nations by the gross underdevelopment of education—widespread illiteracy, lack of schools and teachers,
particularly at the secondary level—and insufficient attention to practical technical skills. Of course, facilities for
higher education are even more restricted, but here, paradoxically enough, because of traditional personal goals
there is sometimes an overproduction of frustrated intellectuals unwilling to soil their hands with manual work
and a dearth of engineers and technicians capable of
contributing practically to national development.

Consequently, there is a woeful shortage of infrastructure, roads and other utilities, hospitals and low-cost
housing—all of those elements of the economy which are
not subject to profitable investment but which are indispensable to a viable and progressive society. There is a
natural and needful demand for industrialization, which
cannot begin to be met but which nevertheless too often
results in grandiose projects at the expense of even more
urgently necessary agricultural development. Agriculture
is often unbalanced, with a serious underproduction of
proteins, consequent nutritional deficiencies, and sometimes irreversible damage to the potentialities of children.
The "green revolution"—the invention of "miracle"
grains doubling and tripling traditional yields—has produced extraordinary results, but it is costly and has not
been applied widely enough, and where it is applied
sometimes has very damaging side effects. In fact it is
already clear that the "miracle" cannot go on forever,
because it is already discernible that there is an eventual
inflexible ceiling on the amount of food that can be
produced by any means without placing intolerable strain,

direct or indirect, on the environment essential to human survival.

Earlier, I referred to high unemployment in cities, but this is a plague which infects and weakens the whole society of developing nations. In some countries as much as 20 or 30 percent of the labor force is out of work, and the figures are often even higher for young people who often make up more than half of the population. As Pearson has said, "The failure to create meaningful employment is the most tragic failure of development."

Finally, there is almost always an extreme shortage of domestic capital, and what there is has to be squeezed in large part from the poverty-stricken peasant mass of the population. Hence, foreign capital is desperately needed and ardently sought. However, because of the experience of past exploitation and the appeal of Marxist clichés, there is an abiding suspicion that foreign capital represents "economic colonialism" or "neo-imperialism." This attitude is particularly directed toward foreign private capital, which indeed has all too often been mainly concerned with drawing profits out of the country rather than reinvesting them in it. Similar suspicions, moreover, often affect foreign aid from a great power, which it is feared may be attempting to impose thereby a veiled political domination, or at least to extract concessions incompatible with the new nation's sovereignty. Hence, among these countries there is an acute ambivalence about foreign aid, reflected on the one hand by an almost universal demand on the developed countries that they devote 1 percent of their GNP annually to foreign aid; reflected on the other hand by the widespread nationalization of private foreign investments and indignant rejection of proffered public aid which seems to have "strings attached."

These problems in regard to aid and investment are further complicated by the large supervisory staffs which donor countries insist on imposing on the recipient to assure themselves that the aid is not being wasted; such personnel are practically required by their mandate to "interfere in internal affairs." An even graver complication, which should long ago have been foreseen, arises from the fact that over the past decade and a half, aid has increasingly been in the form of loans rather than grants. In many countries huge debts have been accumulated which often can never be repaid and the mere servicing of which at the present time sometimes absorbs as much as a third of the debtor government's annually available foreign exchange. A recent example of the political consequences of such a situation was the overthrow in Ghana in January 1972 of a democratically elected civilian government which had endeavored, by imposing an austerity program, to find domestic resources necessary to service huge debts extravagantly incurred years before by the dictator Nkrumah.

A final obstacle to the growth of capital and foreign exchange in developing countries is the normally unfavorable character of the terms of trade. Their imports are largely manufactured goods whose prices are rising, whereas their exports are primarily raw materials often in surplus and hence subject to sharply falling prices. Frequently the fall of a cent or two in the price of coffee, cocoa or rubber will more than wipe out all the foreign aid a country has received over a span of years. Moreover, when a developing country does at last begin to export manufactured goods, the developed countries, fearing cheap competition for their producers, are all too likely to erect trade barriers which stifle or sharply curtail these imports. The slogan "Trade, not aid" therefore often seems to developing nations to be a gross deception, and in practice, promised preferences on their behalf often vanish into thin air.

Such, in summary exposition, is the human condition of 70 percent of the nations and well over half of the population of the world. The condition of these peoples is still, in Hobbes' famous phrase, "poor, nasty, brutish and short." It has no doubt always been so, but now, in sharp contradiction to the past, it is accompanied by passionately rising expectations of betterment, as well as by a conviction, no doubt premature but no less intense, that in view of the triumphs of modern technology, this "brutish" condition is no longer necessary or tolerable. The destitute inhabitant of an Asian or Latin American shantytown sees—not only in movies and magazines from abroad but in the conspicuous consumption of foreigners and privileged indigenous minorities—irrefutable evidence of the superabundant wealth that modern technology pours out so lavishly. His ambitious and not always prudent political leaders assure him that this wealth can and will be available to him as well. Fortified by the legitimate claims thus generated, these leaders thereupon demand of the developed nations that the gross inadequacies between rich and poor nations be promptly corrected, and that the blessings of the affluent society be no longer confined to Europe, North America and tempting islands of privilege elsewhere.

A world where these conditions and expectations confront each other so dramatically and so universally can no longer be stable and safe even for the richest countries and peoples. Unless there is gradual but perceptible improvement in and among the developing nations, before long they are likely to become so morbidly inflamed that they will infect the rest of the globe.

Now I turn to the behavior of the great powers in regard to these nations, commencing with a few general observations and then offering specific illustrations in Europe, Latin America, Asia, the Middle East and Africa.

Great powers are ambivalent about the Third World. At times they simply wish it would go away and relieve them of the burdens of responsibility and guilt which its existence entails. How comfortable the world might be if the poor were not always with us! At other times the big nations are stirred to action by their inclination to exert power and draw benefits from an area with valuable resources, or by their fear that if they do not someone else will. This motive has been heightened by the Cold War, and accounts for most of the damaging and some of the beneficial interventions in the Third World during the past quarter century.

In all fairness it should be emphasized at the outset that the most significant action of the developed vis-à-vis the developing nations in recent years has been the vast commitment of aid of many kinds—far greater and more disinterested than any prospect of profit or power could explain. That the effort has been insufficient is clear, but that it has been massive and admirable is equally obvious. The record of the ex-colonial states, such as Britain and France, particularly in regard to their former colonies, has been especially outstanding. Only poverty-stricken Portugal, at enormous cost to itself, has persisted in pretending to be an empire in the age of decolonization.

The performance of the United States in regard to both developmental and humanitarian aid has also on the whole been exemplary, though from the beginning it has suffered from a mixture of motives which has confused us as well as everyone else. We naïvely supposed that aid would confer on its recipients the blessing of democracy; that it would be administered with an impeccable honesty and efficiency unknown in our own large cities; that it would stifle the spread of Communism, or even neutralism; that it would buy votes in the United Nations.

Having learned that in no case would it do all these things and in some cases not do any, we have become disillusioned and disgruntled, and, while spending $880 million a year on cosmetics and $80 billion a year on liquor and automobiles, we now talk of placing the rest of the world on an austerity budget. Our expectation of how far developing nations could progress in two decades was almost as extravagant as theirs. There is a generation gap between us, and we find it as frustrating not to be able to choose their future for them as for our own children.

The Soviets have been even more ambivalent and much less generous than we have. Of course, they have less to be generous with, and their own underprivileged consumers take a very dim view of making sacrifices for Arabs and Indians. But Soviet citizens have little to say about what happens to their resources, and their leaders have distributed military and economic largesse to poorer countries whenever they thought it politically or ideologically profitable. Still, the Soviet Union has had no better luck than the United States in molding the Third World to its heart's desire. Outside of Southeast Asia, where the costs have been enormous, and Cuba, which is an unreliable satellite, Communism has not gained an inch in twenty-five years; nor have flirtations with fellow travelers like Sukarno, Nkrumah, Lumumba or Ben Bella proved rewarding.

Now the People's Republic of China, with even less resources but somewhat more acceptable credentials in the eyes of the developing nations, has entered the lists to compete for the inheritance of Marx and Lenin. This competition will be fascinating to observe and will no doubt be momentarily profitable to some developing nations, but it could prove as dangerous to the peace of the world as was the Cold War between less fraternal powers.

How do the great and near-great powers manage their benevolence and their intrusions in the Third World? The instruments of both largesse and competition are abundantly diverse, though actually they differ from those used by the precocious states of the Renaissance only in magnitude. There are military alliances, pacts or guarantees of varying degrees of precision and commitment. There are programs of military assistance, including not only in some cases the most sophisticated weapons but also thousands of "advisers" and "technicians" shading off imperceptibly into participants in combat. There are economic programs directly related to development or relief, and others designed for "defense support"—that is, to enable the recipient to devote an otherwise unacceptable part of its own resources to maintaining armed forces. There is a bewildering assortment of more or less covert activities, ranging from legitimate and illegitimate intelligence gathering to the clandestine mobilization and support of substantial military operations, to the buying of elections and the organization of coups d'état against "unreliable" regimes. There are the encouragement and protection of private investment, for the most part genuinely concerned with private profit only, but welcomed by the government of the country of origin both as helping to create a proper political climate in the country where the investment is placed, as well as reducing the need for official aid. There is the composite apparatus of propaganda comprising radio broadcasts, information centers, magazines and films, libraries, public and private press services, and the legal or illegal proselytism carried on by "fraternal" political parties. Finally, there is the central political orchestration of this heterogeneous effort by foreign ministries and embassies—though this orchestration is often frustrated by confusion of policy, disparity of aims among policy-makers and insubordination of agencies and instruments.

Needless to say, this complex apparatus of intrusion has produced vigorous if ambivalent reactions among developing countries. Some, peculiarly sensitive to threats to their sovereignty or "nonalignment," and shocked either by the influence a major aid-donor acquires in their own political structure or by the struggles within it provoked by competition between two or more donors, eventually send the intruders packing and manage as best they can with what they can extract from international institutions. Others cynically provoke competition among donors and balance them off against each other, pursuing (usually with diminishing returns) the most from both possible worlds. Still others, generally those most threatened by external or internal enemies, attach themselves firmly to one camp or another and over time parlay their loyalty into fantastic amounts and varieties of aid.

In these latter cases one sees one of the most curious phenomena of modern international politics: the autonomy and power of intrinsically weak client states. Once such a state has attached itself firmly to a particular donor, has sought and obtained a massive military and economic aid program, has become a conspicuous arena of struggle between global powers and ideologies, and has thus constructed a committed constituency in the power structure of the donor country, the government of the client state becomes—if it plays its cards cleverly—practically invulnerable to the influence and pressure of the theoretically all-powerful donor. At the slightest suggestion of such pressure the client government piously wraps itself in the mantle of sovereignty and declares that it will never tolerate imposed settlements or interference, even by cherished friends, in its internal affairs. The donor, no matter how legitimate its demands for internal reforms essential to the success of the joint enterprise or for reasonable concessions necessary to a peaceful external settlement, finds its apparently overwhelming leverage to be almost valueless. In theory it could enforce its will by withholding or reducing aid, but in practice, while often threatening or even attempting to do so, it soon finds it has committed so much of its own prestige to the success and loyalty of the client that it dare not risk jeopardizing either. If the donor *really* applied effective sanctions against a stubborn client, it might bring about the latter's downfall and replacement by one less loyal or capable, might undermine the joint operation and so tip adversely the global equilibrium, or might so enrage a powerful constituency of the client inside the donor state that the political leadership there could be badly hurt.

So in 1914 Austria and Serbia took almost unilaterally

the fateful decisions that dragged Germany, Russia, France and Britain into World War I. So in recent times governments in Nanking, Seoul, Taiwan, Saigon and Tel Aviv, apparently wholly dependent on American aid for survival, have repeatedly and brazenly defied the United States over policies, reform or settlements it sought to carry out, and yet have managed to obtain from it ever more massive support and assistance.

Competition in, about and among less developed countries can be abundantly illustrated from recent history in various parts of the world.

The Soviet Union's foreign policy since World War II has been largely determined by its obsession with maintaining its control in Eastern Europe, for reasons related most to national security and fear of Germany and the West but also colored by ideological commitments, habits and instruments. For the sake of Eastern Europe Russia sacrificed even a shadow of postwar cooperation with the United States, launched the Cold War and grossly distorted its domestic priorities and evolution over at least the next three decades. The only means it found sufficiently reliable for its purpose was total domination through a combination of satellite political parties, tight police surveillance and military presence. Even this elaborate machinery proved insufficient to prevent the defection of Yugoslavia and Albania. Fear of similar consequences from milder manifestations of independence in Hungary and Czechoslovakia prompted massive military intervention to maintain control.

After 1947 the Western powers tacitly admitted their impotence beyond the eastern boundaries of West Germany, Austria, Yugoslavia and Greece. Yet even east of this line the Soviets could maintain their hegemony only by crude military force, and even under its shadow, ingenious leaders of East Germany, Rumania, Poland and Hungary successfully exploited the leverage of the weak to work toward some of their separate national goals. One might conclude that even a ruthless superpower can reliably control an underdeveloped area only where its armed forces can intervene massively without fear of provoking global conflict, and that, even here, control is never perfect or certain.

In Latin America, the roughly comparable region adjacent to the other superpower, the United States has neither the reason nor the inclination to exercise such control or to intervene substantially. Such pretensions were abandoned with the adoption of Roosevelt's Good Neighbor policy forty years ago and replaced by a series of multilateral treaties based on the sovereign equality of the parties. However, there are limitations to this posture of restraint, of which the most obvious is resistance to the establishment of the other superpower in the area. Castro was firmly entrenched, as the ill-conceived and misconducted episode of the Bay of Pigs demonstrated, before his apostasy from the "American system" became apparent. But as the missile crisis a year later equally showed, the Soviets were not to be permitted to exploit their American satellite for military purposes. Moreover, leftist governments in Guatemala and the Dominican Republic were eased out by clandestine or overt intervention, and others elsewhere were more subtly eroded.

However, Latin America's identity crisis, its social and political modernization, and its consequent growing ambivalence toward the United States may be expected to reach a kind of climax during the next decade or two. Premonitory symptoms are already particularly visible in Chile and Peru. More revolutionary regimes, less often Marxist than populist, more often military than civilian, usually combining socialism and nationalism, can be expected to take over in more and more countries. Neglected and oppressed majorities will become even more numerous, more urbanized, more hungry, more desperate and less manageable. Governments will feel entitled to —and will demand—more assistance from the United

States, but will be less willing either to accept conditions attached to intergovernmental aid or to permit private investment to operate with its customary independence of local control. There could easily be an epidemic of nationalization of such investments despite loud threats of retaliation from Washington. The United States will be baffled, affronted and outraged by many of these phenomena, and will be tempted to react by reducing rather than expanding aid, trade and investment, and by furiously dismantling rather than realistically modifying multilateral political arrangements.

If we do so, we are almost certain to provoke equally emotional and compulsive reactions from our Latin friends, including new agreements and arrangements with each other, with the Russians and with the Chinese. A proliferation of Cubas around the Americas—if it went that far—would be likely to provoke in the United States the most acute apprehensions and passionate responses, not excluding covert and overt intervention. In this way, without any of those involved planning or wishing it, the clock of inter-American relations could be turned back fifty years—but this time in the new and hazardous climate of the nuclear age. Under these circumstances the problems of the Soviet Union with Eastern Europe could come to seem insignificant in comparison with those of the United States with its one-time "good neighbors."

The most abused, beset and embattled part of the Third World during the past century has been East Asia, where, prior to World War II, only Japan was able to resist successfully the encroachments of the West. From 1842 to 1949 China did not have a government which was master in its own house, and indeed only in the last few years has the government of the People's Republic obtained general international recognition. It will be many decades before that century of impotence and humiliation is forgotten by the Chinese. Even now, the People's Republic believes itself to be deprived of a part of its national territory,

Taiwan, and to be confronted on four sides by three actively or potentially intrusive great powers: the Soviet Union, the United States and Japan. For some time its foreign policy will understandably be conditioned by its sense of this deprivation and these dangers.

The relationship of China, the most underdeveloped of the great powers, to the other underdeveloped nations of the world, remains enigmatic, like so much that is Chinese. The fears which obsessed the United States for two decades after 1950—that China would by overt or covert means subjugate her weaker neighbors, even India—have largely though not wholly evaporated. It is now primarily the Soviet Union which fears from China a competition in the Third World compounded of Marxist heterodoxy, more militant and cunning subversion and economic assistance on outrageously generous terms. In actual fact, neither Chinese capabilities nor intentions in these respects may prove as competitive as both the Soviets and the West have supposed. While continuing to claim that capitalism, imperialism and "revisionism" are doomed, and that they will never be indifferent to the process by which this end is gloriously achieved, the Chinese stress that each people must by its own efforts make its own revolution. No doubt they will be willing to assist modestly, but so far they are creating no illusions that even in weak, embattled countries close at hand they will play a decisive role. From their newly acquired seat in the United Nations, while denouncing the Soviet Union and the United States they are piously disclaiming any pretension of being a superpower, and staunchly pro- claiming the inviolability of national sovereignty. Maoist like Imperial China still seems likely, for some years at least, to be the most self-centered and self-absorbed of all peoples and powers.

None of the smaller nations on the periphery of China—Korea, the Philippines, Vietnam, Laos, Cambodia, Indonesia, Malaysia, Singapore and Burma—have come

even close to achieving economic and social modernization, political stability and confident national identity.
Two—Korea and Vietnam—were artificially divided by
external powers, and then the two halves were, thanks
largely to these same powers, brought into a hostile
confrontation against each other which still persists. This
is intervention of a particularly extreme and painful kind.
Indeed, since 1945 the whole region has become, in
varying degrees, an arena for the East–West struggle—first
in China itself, then Korea, then Vietnam, Laos and
Cambodia, and more indigenously but still cruelly, Indonesia, Malaysia and Burma. Twice one of the great
powers, the United States, has been massively involved in
prolonged combat in East Asia, while the Soviet Union
and China with men or weapons massively supported the
other side. Even Japan, the strongest and most auton-
omous of the nations of the area, is ambivalent about its
role and future, and baffles both itself and others as to
what it may do when it finally reasserts itself.

What is most striking, most destabilizing and most
intolerable over the long run is that so many of the major
decisions about the fate of the area—war and peace, life
and death—in Korea, Vietnam, Laos and Cambodia, have
been made by people living thousands of miles away.
Some of the most ancient portions of mankind have for
many years been objects and victims of other people's
foreign policy rather than being sovereign subjects and
beneficiaries of their own. Villages are wiped out in order
to "save" them; millions of men, women and children are
moved about like cattle time after time; war is prolonged
year after year when those most concerned, if left alone,
could and would have made peace. Here, most grossly and
most unpardonably, the great powers, from the depths of
their ignorance and the height of their pride, have presumed to impose *their* justice and *their* creeds on peoples
at least as civilized as themselves.

The Indian subcontinent contains still another immense

accumulation of human beings, embracing a riotous diversity of ethnic, linguistic, religious and political elements, including some of the richest and many of the most miserable, some of the most sophisticated and many of the most primitive of mankind. For all its faults, the British Empire imposed upon this vast domain and its peoples the benefits of unity and representative government which India at least has so far preserved. However, in 1947 the subcontinent itself was tragically and foolishly split on traditional lines. Pakistan was artificially created in the form of a geographic monstrosity, and Kashmir was left dangling as a bone of contention between the two. Now Pakistan has been partitioned and Bangladesh, a new state of uncertain viability, created. All three states are confronted with enormous problems of demography, hunger, economic underdevelopment, urban overconcentration and political tensions. No one can predict from year to year whether any of the three can maintain its unity and territorial integrity, whether they can resolve their differences and coexist peacefully, whether in the foreseeable future they can play the significant role in the world to which their population, resources and level of civilization entitle them, or whether they can resist renewed intrusions from outside.

So far they cannot complain too much on the latter score. They have been recipients of enormous amounts of economic and military assistance from both West and East, which both India and Pakistan have been remarkably successful in playing off against each other. India was greatly helped in its military victory over Pakistan in December 1971 by the support of the Soviet Union. Yet for the most part they have been too large and powerful to be manipulated by outsiders. Should they weaken or disintegrate, this would not necessarily continue to be the case. The more fiercely and violently they confront each other, the more they will need and probably receive military aid from outside—India from the Soviet Union,

Pakistan from China, and perhaps both from the West—and the more they will thus stimulate great-power intrusion and rivalry in their region.

One such source of danger is the possible transformation of the hitherto peaceful Indian Ocean into an area of naval rivalry between the Soviet Union and the United States. Such a confrontation so far from the territory and so unrelated to the essential interests of either superpower would be absurd, but this will not necessarily prevent it from happening. If they wish to insulate the ocean from rivalries and confrontations wholly alien to them, the nations of the whole Indian Ocean basin would be well advised to deny access to their ports to all warships of non-riparian states. However, if India and Pakistan have made themselves dependent on such states for arms directed at each other, they would have difficulty agreeing to deny these states access to their ocean.

Another critical Third World area which since World War I has been liberated, fragmented and radicalized, and has suffered and profited from a variety of foreign intrusions, is the Middle East. Its northern tier—Greece, Turkey and Iran—was for some time a front line between East and West, and has taken advantage of Western concern on this score, as well as of its own human and natural resources, to make impressive progress on the road to economic and political modernization. The Arab world, on the other hand, has been plagued by Anglo-French interventions from 1919 to 1956, and by Soviet–American rivalry since that time. Further, it has been divided within by traditionalists, modernizers and revolutionaries, has been broken up into a welter of medium, small and very small states reaching from Kuwait to Morocco, and most of all, has been polarized and agonized by its failure either to expel, accept or adjust to the triumphant anachronism that is the state of Israel.

Partly as a consequence of the Soviet's ambition to leap

over the northern tier and contest the West's domination of the Eastern Mediterranean, partly as a curious by-product of the Arab–Israeli conflict, the Middle East has become a critical point of possible military confrontation between the two superpowers. The oddly contradictory result has been both the extravagant arming by each of its chosen client and the joint efforts, so far frustrated by the passions and fears of the clients, to find a solution to the conflict.

As U.S. Ambassador to the UN, I took part for two years in almost weekly meetings of the Four Powers concerned—the United States, the USSR, the United Kingdom and France—in an effort to find or facilitate a settlement in the Middle East. I believe that all four genuinely wished and sought agreement. Though the Arab–Israeli conflict had provided the means for their intrusion into the area, even the Soviets were sufficiently fearful of renewed and uncontrollable warfare between the two sides—through which they might themselves be drawn into direct confrontation with the United States—to prefer settlement to an unstable truce. Moreover, the Four Powers could with relative ease have agreed on a settlement acceptable to themselves and, in their view, just to both parties. But Israel and the Arab states most concerned would have none of it, and their views, not those of the big powers, prevailed. After the death of Nasser, Cairo, it is true, offered what had been so long sought—a peace agreement with Israel—but by that time Israel had decided that her security could be safeguarded only by territorial expansion well beyond her June 1967 frontiers. Neither side would move enough, and each preferred to blame the other for failure than to risk the internal political complications which mutual concession and common success would have required.

So each of the superpowers continued docilely to supply its client with the lavish assortment of arms which both demanded and neither needed, despite the almost insolent disregard of its patron's proposals and interests which each of the clients continued to display. It can only be concluded that until the states of the area decide to reassert their autonomy effectively by coming to terms with each other, or until the great powers themselves decide that the risks of disengagement are less than those of deeper involvement, the Middle East will remain for the great powers a fuse to general war and for its inhabitants a battleground instead of a Promised Land.

One rather ominous footnote needs to be added to this discussion of the Middle East. The economic life of the developed nations substantially depends, and will do so for some time to come, on oil, of which a very large proportion comes from a group of developing nations associated in the Organization of Petroleum Exporting Countries. The members of OPEC are Saudi Arabia, Iran, Iraq, Kuwait, Qatar, Abu Dhabi, Libya, Algeria, Nigeria, Indonesia and Venezuela. Of the eleven, eight are in the Middle East or North Africa. At present these eleven countries supply about 87 percent of Western Europe's oil and about 80 percent of Japan's. They now supply only 17 percent of U.S. requirements, but it is estimated in the industry that by 1980 they may be supplying 30 percent. Moreover, while at present most of OPEC's oil resources are "owned" in large part by U.S. or West European corporations, the governments of OPEC countries have already made it clear that they will soon insist on at least minority participation in ownership, followed probably in a decade or so by majority participation. In point of fact they already have the power to nationalize, as the Libyan government has done with British Petroleum, or to limit or even embargo exports.

Unless other sources of oil or of energy can be developed far more rapidly than is now believed possible, these eleven developing nations, perhaps joined by other smaller producers, can exert enormous pressure on the oil-hungry industrial countries. Their present primary objective is to obtain a larger share of the revenues, and it is therefore in their interest as well as that of the consumers that the flow of oil continue and increase. Sad experience has often shown, however, that nations of diverse cultures and goals have varying conceptions of what constitutes "national interest." At any time Arab states might decide, contrary to their apparent economic interest, to manipulate oil supplies to the West in order to put pressure indirectly on Israel to evacuate Arab territories—or simply to retaliate against Western countries which are helping Israel to keep these territories. Alternatively, increasingly heated and emotional arguments over division of profits or participation in ownership could lead to widespread nationalization. Therefore, political confrontation during the present decade between the oil-producing nations of the Middle East and the developed nations dependent on this oil seems all too probable, and the consequences could be extremely damaging to all concerned.

The "newest" part of the Third World—though it may be man's oldest habitat—is Africa. At the outbreak of World War II it could boast of only three more or less independent nations: Liberia, Egypt and South Africa. It now has forty. Their liberation is welcome and long overdue, but their number is excessive. The continent was Balkanized by the rivalry of the colonial powers whose African territories were carved out with little reference to either ethnic or economic realities. As a consequence few of the new states have by themselves the resources, internal cohesion or sense of national identity to develop rapidly or to play a substantial role in the world community. Yet their leaders are reluctant to attempt to revise the boundaries drawn by colonialism, lest they plunge into the sort of internecine wars which so long and uselessly disrupted Europe.

Federation would in many cases be the sensible answer, but elites newly established even on narrow and uncomfortable seats of power are reluctant to share them with others. The elites themselves are for the most part young, inexperienced and insecure. Some are doctrinaire intellectuals unhappily obliged to be pragmatists; others are pragmatic traditionalists unhappily obliged to profess racial or ideological dogmas; many are young military men without ideological commitment or interests of any kind. They are further split between speakers of English, French and Arabic who, too often reflecting the Anglo-Saxon, Gallic or Moslem biases in which they were educated, find great difficulty cooperating effectively even in the so-called Organization of African Unity or in the United Nations.

The principal common goal of these new states is the liberation of the black peoples still under Portuguese, South African and Rhodesian domination. But since they do not have the means or the will to achieve this end alone, at the moment this shared purpose serves mainly as a source of discord between them and the Western powers, and, for the Communists, as an excuse for intervention in Southern African affairs.

During the past dozen years since the majority of African states have gained independence, external intervention there has been limited and on the whole beneficent. The unity of the Congo was preserved, and a further spiral of Balkanization prevented, by the United Nations in one of its most effective peace-keeping operations. Similarly the unity of the most populous African state, Nigeria, was maintained with the support of both Western and Eastern powers, though the French could not resist the temptation to weaken the Anglophones by aiding the bloody Biafran revolt. Economic aid and investment in Africa have been extensive but not large, except in especially profitable oil and minerals and by the French and British in their former territories. For both strategic and economic reasons, the southern littoral of the Mediterranean already attracts intense great-power interest and could provoke their involvement if the states of the area are not alert to draw the line between aid and intervention.

The real focus of potential catastrophe is, however, Southern Africa where thirty-five million blacks are still anachronistically ruled and in some cases grievously oppressed by white minorities, ranging from 19 percent of the population in South Africa to 5 percent in Rhodesia. If this anomaly is not corrected gradually and peacefully, it will be corrected suddenly and hideously in years to come. Moreover, far from being bulwarks against Communism, as the white governments claim to be, it is their inflexible adherence to immobility and apartheid which offer the best opportunity for the establishment of eventually triumphant Communist movements in Africa.

During the decade of the 1960's when I served at the United Nations, African ambassadors would often ask me whether violence and bloodshed was the only way they could attract and hold our attention, the only means of getting sufficient help to resolve their problems. On the basis of my experience I am convinced that without strong outside pressure these problems are not going to be solved peacefully and progressively by the whites of these areas. The status quo is far too comfortable. Furthermore, if the problems are left to be resolved eventually by violence, there will be a ghastly repetition of what took place in 1971 in East Pakistan—with the additional complication in this case of far-reaching and traumatic black-vs.-white overtones.

Over the past dozen years the United Nations has again and again taken action designed to correct or improve this situation. Sanctions have been imposed on Rhodesia, arms embargoes have been applied to South Africa and Portugal, countless resolutions have been passed denouncing apartheid and calling for self-determination and freedom for the black majorities. None of these actions seem to have had the slightest effect on the white minority governments. On the contrary, it is the UN measures which, as they are increasingly abandoned by the United States, the United Kingdom and France among others, are falling apart. The United States frankly is still trying to do the

minimum that would appease the forty African governments without seriously incommoding its Portuguese and
South African friends or the U.S. corporations with investments there. Politically this seems the easy way, but in the
end it will not work. Someday Southern Africa will be
shockingly and hideously on the front pages of the world
press. Then the Western powers will ask themselves why
they did not, with all the nonmilitary resources at their
command, push and drive South Africa, Rhodesia and
Portugal into the modern world while there was still time.

In conclusion, it may be said about all these regions of
the Third World—Latin America, East Asia, the Indian
subcontinent, the Middle East and Africa—that their
problems are so new and so vast, their conflicts, tensions
and needs so great, the temptations they offer to the great
powers so irresistible, that no existing machinery of the
international community is capable of dealing effectively
with them. They themselves cannot do so separately; their
regional organizations are far too weak, and there is not
likely soon to be any concert of great powers sufficiently
disinterested, cohesive and single-minded to do so. Even
the United Nations is still denied by the developed
countries the authority and resources to cope effectively.
Yet if no sufficient means can soon be devised to meet the
elementary needs and resolve the compulsive fears of
two-thirds of mankind, the last quarter of the twentieth
century is likely to be as dreadfully and futilely violent for
us all as were the first three.

In this section I have examined and reflected upon a
number of causes of disorientation in the conduct of
foreign affairs: disorientation arising from domestic
factors; disorientation arising from creeds, ideologies and
crusades; disorientation arising from the personal psychology of powerful leaders; disorientation arising from
military obsessions; and finally disorientation caused by
the sudden juxtaposition, alongside the older powers of

northern Europe, Asia and America, of almost a hundred new states—unsure of their identity or their fate.

I now turn to a closer examination of the instruments employed by governments for the management of foreign affairs, particularly those deployed over recent decades by the United States, the strongest superpower.

The Foreign-Affairs Apparatus in the United States: Its Management and Mismanagement

The President   The U.S. Presidency is, at least among great powers, a unique institution. In the most powerful of the democracies the chief of state has at his disposal more power inside his own government than his counterpart in any large state, including the dictatorships. Even Brezhnev could not have gone to war in Vietnam without the consent of the Politburo. In order to oust Liu Shao-chi and his "running dogs," Mao had to recess school for four years and mobilize the entire youth of the land against the bureaucracy he himself had established. To be sure, an American President can lose "the mandate of heaven," as Wilson and Johnson did, but until he does so, his power over foreign affairs is nearly unlimited.

For this reason, the central question about the management of foreign affairs in the United States has not been, despite occasional short-lived revolts in the Congress, what authority the President should have, but how and through whom he should exercise it. In the earlier section on the psychology of leaders I discussed some aspects of the conduct of foreign affairs by the last six American Presidents. In a sense the whole discussion of the foreign-affairs apparatus in this section will reflect the will of

Presidents because each of them, while his ability to formally reorganize departments of the government is subject to the consent of Congress, can in fact use or not use, exalt or diminish, each of the components of his own administration more or less as he chooses. Even a desperately ill President, such as Wilson in his last eighteen months, could so effectively wield power from his bedroom that no one other than himself could conduct foreign affairs for the United States during that decisive time.

This recalls Dean Acheson's remark, quoted earlier, that a President cannot in practice be his own Secretary of State because he has another job to do, but that he can if he chooses, prevent anyone else from being Secretary of State. Despite the seeming obviousness of this fact, many Presidents have tried in one way or another to be their own Secretaries of State. The results have not been happy.

At least from 1940 onward Roosevelt apparently acted in the belief that diplomacy was too serious a matter to be left to the diplomats. Of course, he had created a major obstacle for himself in the character of the Secretary of State he appointed and kept in office for nearly twelve years. Cordell Hull was an eminently honest man and nobody's fool, but nothing in his experience or bent of mind prepared him for being in charge of the foreign affairs of a great power at one of the most critical moments in its history. But while bypassing Hull as much as he could, even Roosevelt at first placed his own men, on whom he did to some extent rely, inside the State Department itself: Sumner Welles and later Edward Stettinius as Undersecretaries; Raymond Moley and Adolph Berle as Assistant Secretaries; and William Bullitt and Joseph Kennedy as ambassadors. On the other hand, after war came, Roosevelt almost wholly excluded the Department from decision-making, and insofar as he took advice at all on foreign-policy matters, took it from the military, Harry Hopkins and the heads of new emergency agencies.

Thus, for largely personal and accidental reasons, a

precedent was set, during the critical period of U.S. emergence as a superpower, for bypassing the Secretary of State and the Foreign Service, and for diffusing the conduct of foreign affairs at home and abroad among a wide and constantly changing complex of agencies. An even more unfortunate precedent set at the same time was, as described earlier, the persistent and intimate involvement of the military in foreign-policy decision-making, natural enough in wartime but creating in peacetime an imbalance of judgment toward military instruments and solutions which has distorted U.S. foreign policy over twenty-five years. These developments arose not from any need to confirm or strengthen the authority of the President in the conduct of foreign affairs, which was never challenged, but simply from the sudden pressures of an abnormal situation, the personal style of a particular President, and the limitations of a particular Secretary of State.

Fortunately, Truman lacked Roosevelt's egregious over-estimate of his capacity to conduct foreign affairs single-handed. He appointed three strong Secretaries of State—Byrnes, Marshall and Acheson—and, while Byrnes presumed too much upon this *modus operandi* and was dismissed, it worked extremely well with Marshall and Acheson. Moreover, Truman set up no machinery which could act as a barrier between him and his Secretaries, and permitted no other agency of government to defy or evade their authority over foreign policy and its implementation. When a Secretary of Defense, Louis Johnson, appeared to do so, he was promptly removed. This simple, workman-like system provided a basis for the successful conduct of our foreign affairs during the decisive phase of our post-war history.

Eisenhower preserved more or less intact the system and procedures his predecessor had followed. He appointed a strong Secretary of State in whom he had full confidence, and entrusted him consistently with the main responsibility for the formulation and implementation of foreign policy. Again there was no question that the President was Commander in Chief, but there was also no question that John Foster Dulles was his sole chief of staff for foreign affairs. Whatever one may think of its policies, under this Administration the U.S. government spoke with a single firm clear voice abroad.

The next three Presidents, without particularly solid grounds in my view, all considered themselves experts in foreign affairs and each desired to be his own Secretary of State. All of them, moreover, for different personal reasons had little respect for the career Foreign Service. These predilections and antipathies had several unfortunate consequences from the point of view of the conduct of foreign affairs and, in my opinion, of the protection of the national interest.

In the first place, the two Secretaries of State of the period, Dean Rusk and William Rogers, were allowed little initiative and latitude; when they were, it was chiefly in areas of lesser interest to the President. Second, the three Presidents built up separate directorates of foreign affairs in the White House, headed by men of outstanding ability but without the depth and breadth of experience in the foreign field which might have saved them from some of the blunders into which they stumbled—Indochina being the most significant. Third, while they did not augment the already overinflated role of the military in foreign-policy formulation, these three Presidents and their two Secretaries were less able to put military advice in perspective than Eisenhower, and less willing to insist on the prerogatives of the Department than Acheson and Dulles.

President Kennedy was extremely impatient of what he considered the bureaucratic involution and inertia of the State Department and had a habit of phoning bureau chiefs or their subordinates to spur them on to action. During the Laotian crisis at the beginning of his Administration, it was said that the desk officer for Laos was the President of the United States. It is reported that he once asked Charles Bohlen, one of the ablest and most experienced of Foreign Service officers, "What's the matter with your Department?" To which Bohlen replied, "You are, Mr. President." Bohlen may have meant either that the President had failed to permit the Secretary of State to act with sufficient authority and efficiency, or that the President and his White House staff were involving themselves too deeply in the implementation of policy. The process by which the Bay of Pigs operation was decided, from which all the knowledgable people in the State Department were wholly excluded, was a classic example of how not to conduct foreign affairs.

President Johnson, whose extraordinary legislative talents had not prepared him in any way to administer a vast complex of executive departments and agencies, chose to conduct both foreign and military affairs through an intense, twenty-four-hour-a-day personal involvement, in consultation for the most part only with an inner cabinet of four or five. One of these, it is true, was the Secretary of State, but the President's almost pathological aversion to "leaks," or to any publicity that had not been deviously prefabricated, usually prevented any wide involvement of the State Department beneath the levels of Secretary and Undersecretary until policies had already been decided.

President Nixon believed himself—perhaps more complacently than any President since Roosevelt—to be expert in foreign affairs and hence qualified to be his own Secretary of State. He was, moreover, temperamentally uneasy in the give and take of open debate, and preferred to receive advice either in the anodyne form of "options" among which he could choose in the chaste calm of his chambers, or from single privy counselors whose bent of mind was sympathetic but whose status risked no contest of wills. His prescription for the conduct of foreign affairs—perhaps, indeed, his view of their essential con-

tent—differed remarkably little from those of that fifteenth-century monarch mentioned in the introduction to
this book, Louis XI of France.

I do not find the record of these three Presidents in the
conduct of foreign affairs a brilliant one. Some of the main
reasons for their failures were their own oversimplified
conceptions of world politics (similar, incidentally, to that
of the Communists) as a universal struggle between dark-
ness and light; their excessive reliance on the advice of
military and academic strategists committed to the same
misconceptions; and their reluctance to heed advice from
either experienced diplomats or more down-to-earth politicians who might have been more knowledgeable and
realistic about what could be achieved among mysterious
peoples unfamiliar with the doctrines of Calvin or Mahan.

It is safe to say that American Presidents are rarely
chosen for their sophistication in the conduct of foreign
affairs. They are nominated and elected because of what
the electorate knows or believes to be their domestic
policies, or because of some charismatic image which
transcends policy. Yet such is the fascination and so high
the stakes of what has been called the "game of nations"
that only the wisest or the most modest can resist its
glamour. Even the most presumptuous are obliged to seek
advice and to use instruments for implementing policy,
but the more presumptuous also listen only to advice they
want to hear and use only instruments that are completely
subservient. No system can do a greater disservice to a
President than one which denies him steady access to
dissent. If he is told by his most trusted courtiers only
what he wants to hear, he will be confirmed in his errors
and entrapped in his disasters. Johnson's attitudes on
Vietnam from 1964 to 1968 and Nixon's on India and
Pakistan in 1971 are tragic examples of what flows from
this self-deception. Foreign policy in Washington, particularly since the death of Kennedy, has been made too
much in airless rooms where over and over again everyone
breathes in the same stale fantasies.

In most other long-established governments the head of government almost invariably confides the conduct of foreign affairs to the ministry and the career service, which over a great many years has acquired a special knowledge of the external world and a special expertise in dealing with it. Only in the greatest of democracies, where it is a tradition that every man should be able to do everything, is it presumed that amateurs in the White House, in the State Department and in embassies abroad can do at least as well, and probably better, than those bred to the profession.

The National Security Council and Its Staff   The National Security Council was established in 1947 by an Act of Congress which was primarily designed to bring about unification of the armed services. President Truman reports in his memoirs, however, that in proposing establishment of the Council, he wanted "one top-level permanent setup in the government to concern itself with advising the President on high policy decisions concerning the security of the nation." The Council was intended, he said, to give him "a perpetual inventory of where we stood and where we were going on all strategic questions affecting the national security."*

Truman also noted that the NSC "built a small but highly competent permanent staff which was selected for its objectivity and lack of political ties. It was our plan that the staff should serve as a continuing organization regardless of what administration was in power." While this conception of the NSC staff continued for the most part to prevail until the end of the 1950's, it has been radically altered since that time. First, the staff is no longer "small": in 1948 it comprised about ten persons, in 1953 about twenty-five, about fifty in 1961 and about one hundred

*Harry S Truman, *Memoirs* (New York: Doubleday, 1955).

twenty today. Second, its "executive secretary," as he was known at the outset, an inconspicuous civil servant without "political ties," has been transformed into the President's National Security Adviser, one of the most prestigious policy-makers in Washington; but not one likely to survive a change in administration.

In recent years decision-making in the whole field of foreign affairs has become more and more entangled and distorted in the machinery of the Council. This radical shift of locus occurred because the last three Presidents, as suggested earlier, distrusted the State Department and thought they themselves could better control both foreign and military affairs through an instrument inside the White House.

The hazards of such an arrangement were perceived, only two years after the Council was established, by the authors of a task force report on foreign-affairs organization prepared for the Hoover Commission and submitted to the Congress in 1949. The authors, incidentally, were Harvey Bundy and James Grafton Rogers, both of whom had been Assistant Secretaries of State under Henry Stimson in the early 1930's and the former of whom was the father of McGeorge and William Bundy. Even at that early date, their report noted that the terms of reference of the NSC are "so broad that in the name of security it can and does get into numerous matters of foreign affairs which are strictly not its business."* They also noted that the military were heavily overrepresented in it and that there was "real danger" that it could "slip into a highly improper role." They recommended, therefore, that any aspects of foreign affairs which involved more than one department or agency be dealt with by separate, less structured Cabi-

*Harvey H. Bundy and James Grafton Rogers, *The Organization of the Government for the Conduct of Foreign Affairs,* Task Force Report in Foreign Affairs, prepared for the Commission on the Organization of the Executive Branch of the Government (Washington, D. C.: Government Printing Office, 1949).

net-level committees. In addition, they stipulated that these committees should have "an executive secretary with purely procedural and no substantive powers" who "should not build up a large secretariat," but would draw for staff on the regular agencies.

These prescient warnings were ignored, with consequences and side effects which have been distinctly unfortunate. Sufficient note has already been taken of the overinvolvement of the military in the process of foreign-policy formulation.

A second damaging side effect of the Council's preemption of foreign affairs has been further to complicate and prolong an already tedious and constipated decision-making process. Parkinson's Law is given still another golden opportunity to perform. Matters which have already been subjected to the most exhaustive review in the State Department, and by State with other agencies, are dissected, dismantled and put together all over again by the NSC staff. Often months pass before a crucial decision is finally taken, by which time events have frequently moved so far that the decision is obsolete or irrelevant.

Aspects of the process which contribute to this constipation are the over-elaboration of long-range planning, the rationalization of "conceptual frameworks," and the multiplication of artificial "options." I am a strong believer in long-range planning, of deciding in advance where we want to go and how best to get there; however, a bloated mass of studies on every country and every problem only clogs the policy-making process, consumes interminable hours of the experts' time, and is almost always ignored by the policy-makers. Equally futile is the pursuit of broad and exhilarating conceptions on which policy can be based and which will justify it. For the most part such conceptions turn out to be public-relations rephrasings of conventional wisdom, or rationalizations of more sordid and less avowable objectives. In either case they mislead first the public and then their authors. Finally, the preparation of NSC papers in the form of a series of "options" from which the President can theoretically choose is also misguided in two respects: it misleads the President and his advisers into thinking they have more options than the hard facts warrant, and it deprives the President of clear-cut recommendations from people who usually know much more about the subject than he possibly can. I suspect that this device was designed mainly to enable the National Security Adviser, privately and without unseemly argument, to recommend to the President the option he prefers.

Still a third effect is to undermine the prestige and effectiveness of the Secretary of State and the Foreign Service in the conduct of day-to-day relations with other governments. An adviser spending twelve hours a day in the White House and with easy access to the President can, if the Chief Executive allows him, play more of a part in shaping the structure of foreign policy than a Secretary of State who, confined by his duties in the Department and at meetings overseas, sees the President much less frequently. Foreign ambassadors in Washington and American ambassadors abroad are even at times encouraged to believe they can obtain satisfaction of their requirements more easily from the National Security Adviser than from the Secretary of State. This is both petty and scandalous. One is reminded of the anecdote Blanche Dugdale recounted about an exchange at the Paris Peace Conference between Lord Balfour, then Foreign Secretary, and Philip Kerr (later Lord Lothian), Lloyd George's private secretary, who had a habit of usurping the Foreign Office role. When Balfour asked Kerr whether Lloyd George had read a certain memo, Kerr replied; "I don't think so, but I have." Balfour answered, "Not quite the same thing, is it, Philip—yet?"*

A fourth disadvantage of placing so much of the

*Blanche Dugdale, *Arthur James Balfour* (London: Hutchinson, 1936).

foreign-policy-making process in the White House is to subject it even more acutely to the distortions arising from domestic opinion and politics, the sometimes disastrous effects of which were examined earlier in this book. Of course the President in conducting foreign policy must take these factors fully into account, and he and his domestic advisers in the White House are the proper persons to do so. It is far preferable, however, that appreciations of external situations, and recommendations as to how best to deal with them from the viewpoint of our foreign relations, should come to the President in pure and objective form, uncontaminated by preconceptions about what will be most salable to the American public or what will most contribute to his reelection. This sort of objectivity can be far better supplied by a separate department than by a staff submerged night and day in the politically pressurized climate of the White House.

A final damaging consequence of the transfer of foreign-policy decision-making from State to NSC has been (since the NSC staff is not normally permitted to testify before Congressional committees) to remove this process from Congressional scrutiny, to stimulate Congressional mistrust of the President's behavior and intentions in this field, and to foster quite unnecessarily the politico-constitutional crisis over the conduct of foreign affairs which we are now witnessing. Massive and rhetorically titled written reports on foreign policy from the President and the State Department to Congress are far from bridging the gap between the two branches of government—first, because it can only be bridged by people, not documents; and second, because these documents, no matter how voluminous, contain so little substance that they carry little weight.

On all these counts the diversion of foreign policy from the State Department to an office inside the White House has been a disservice to the national interest. Insofar as it confuses and hampers the conduct of foreign affairs, imposes on the process an unjustified and hazardous military bias, and contributes to embroiling the President in controversy with the Congress, this diversion will also prove to be contrary to the narrower political interests of the President himself.

The fact is that in any organization, public or private, it is never wise nor productive to divide responsibility for managing a single field of activity. If two appointees of the President, the Secretary of State and the National Security Adviser, are each given wide authority in the conduct of foreign affairs, there is certain to be both conflict between them and confusion on the part of foreign governments and of the American Congress and public as to where preponderant responsibility lies. Consequently, policy will lack clarity, consistency and credibility, and its implementation will either shuttle back and forth interminably or take off in several directions at once. Far better, from every point of view, including the President's, to center responsibility in one person and one place. A President has no need to divide in order to rule. Overuse by the President of the Council and its staff reflects lack of confidence either in his principal minister or in himself.

The Secretary and Department of State and the Foreign Service After forty years' experience in the conduct of foreign affairs by the U.S. government my considered judgment is that, while conformity to the following rules does not guarantee wise policy, failure to conform to them frequently produces *unwise* policy and almost guarantees maladroit application of *any* policy, good or bad. The rules are: (1) the formulation of foreign policy and management of foreign affairs should be centralized in a single agency, under the President's firm policy guidance but *outside* the White House; (2) this agency should be the one constitutionally responsible for foreign affairs—the State Department; (3) its authority

over all other agencies in the field should be unambig-
uously stated and consistently sustained by the President;
(4) its responsibilities to the Congress should be scrupu-
lously and ungrudgingly carried out; (5) the public should
be objectively and amply informed at all stages of the
process of policy formulation and implementation.

In order that these rules can be effectively applied, the
Secretary of State must be a man of eminence and experience in whom the President has the fullest confidence, to
whom he is willing to grant considerable latitude, but
with whom he confers nearly every day when both are in
Washington. When either one is absent the Secretary
should report almost daily by phone or cable. No matter
how many other agencies are involved in one way or
another in foreign affairs—and there are a great many—the
Secretary of State must be master in his own house at
home and ambassadors must be masters in their embassies
abroad. Other agencies must be subject to the Secretary's
direction when their functions impinge on his; moreover,
he, not they, must be the judge as to when their functions
do so impinge. In case of irreconcilable policy or jurisdic-
tional differences the President would be the final arbiter.

As suggested earlier, there was never any doubt that
Secretaries Marshall, Acheson and Dulles met these criteria and successfully exercised their authority. As also
suggested, subsequent Presidents have not been ready to
confer such authority on their Secretaries, the Secretaries
have not demanded it, and foreign affairs have been in
substantial part conducted by the Presidents themselves,
by Secretaries of Defense or of the Treasury, by National
Security Advisers or even by Attorneys General. Regardless of the quality of the men so empowered, the results
have shown that practical experience in domestic politics,
big business or academia is often inapplicable to the very
different problems of foreign affairs, and indeed, by creating illusions of comparability, may lure prestigious amateurs into disastrous miscalculations in the foreign en-

vironment. Outstanding examples would be Roosevelt's belief that Stalin could be cajoled into peaceful coexistence, Robert McNamara and Walt Rostow's commitment to military victory in Vietnam, and John Connally's use of the big stick to resolve U.S. economic and financial differences with its best friends.

Just as two hundred years ago it was assumed that anyone of gentle birth was fit to lead an army or at least command a regiment, in the United States it is still today assumed that anyone with political or business competence can conduct our relations with the rest of the world, or at least with a single country. This is the era of the expert everywhere except in the field which in many ways is the most critical.

I must frankly admit that part of the depreciation of experts in this field has occasionally arisen from disorganization of the State Department and narrowness of view in the Foreign Service. In this book, which is written for the general reader and not as a blueprint of administrative reform, it would not be appropriate to make detailed proposals for reorganization of the Department. However, it is relevant to lay down several broad principles which in the author's view should govern such reform. The prescription is not much different from that required for any large organization suffering, as most of them do, from Parkinson's disease (defined as "a nerve disease, characterized by tremors, especially of fingers and hands, rigidity of muscles, slowness of movements and speech, and a masklike, expressionless face") and Parkinson's Law.

Authority in the Department needs to be centralized at the top in eight to ten persons who have a comprehensive view of the whole field, who are in daily consultation with each other and who can make major decisions rapidly. These persons should all be appointees of the incumbent Administration, but about half, including the Secretary, should be representatives of the party in power, experienced in foreign affairs but not professionals, and the other half should be drawn from the career Foreign Service.

The Department should be so organized beneath this high command as best to provide the information, analysis and recommendations they need to make knowledgeably the decisions required of them, and to make, without involving them, the vast number of less important day-to-day decisions which need not come to their attention. It is of almost equal importance that information flow down as well as up, and that those officers, junior as well as senior, who know most about an area be consulted before major decisions concerning it are taken. Failure to do so, based on specious and extravagant regard for secrecy, led to the disaster of the Bay of Pigs and, to some degree, to U.S. overinvolvement in the Vietnam war. Senior officers beneath the high command must be perceptive enough to determine what needs to be referred to the top, responsible enough to act themselves on what does not need to be so referred, and courageous enough to protest, vigorously though privately, if they believe the President or the Secretary of State is about to make a serious mistake.

Reference might be made at this point to the recent fad for what is called "crisis management." This has often meant in practice that when a crisis arises abroad—and there is almost constantly a crisis somewhere—not only is an ad hoc "task force" set up, including most of the senior officers concerned with the area in question, but the President and Secretary themselves are likely to be drawn into the ensuing turmoil, sometimes to the exclusion of almost all other business. This top-level involvement is no doubt justified in a case of such overriding danger as the Cuban missile crisis, but it is not when dealing with the innumerable clashes, coups, incidents and "flaps" with which overofficious modern communications punctuate Washington's days and nights. The fact is that many Presidents and Secretaries, and less exalted officials as well, find an irresistible fascination in performing in dramas of this kind, even essentially trivial ones. The less they know about them the more enthralling they are likely to find them. To the despair of his subordinates, President Johnson was particularly addicted to intimate and compulsive involvement in the minutiae of crises. Most of such involvement is a waste of time, a waste of which Presidents and Secretaries of State can ill afford. Even lesser officials find themselves interminably trapped on task forces which take on a life of their own and divert to post-mortems time and attention which should be devoted to the prenatal care of other problems.

I suggest that what we need is not more crisis management but more crisis neglect. Small ills like pimples are more likely to be inflamed than cured by scratching. Often what is most called for is time for everyone to cool off. The security of the United States would have been better served if the Tonkin Gulf incident had been pigeonholed. In any case, Chief Executives and their senior advisers would do better to devote more of their time to looking ahead, to planning and problem-solving, and in general should let their juniors navigate through the minor turbulence that daily agitates the ship of state.

In this connection, an indispensable feature of the State Department should be a planning council which constantly reexamines the long-term goals of foreign policy and studies the implications for those goals of current policy and action. To function effectively for these ends, such a council needs to be unencumbered with current operations but sufficiently close to them so that it is not isolated or ignored. This mix is best achieved when its director is one of the top command and is close to the Secretary—as were, for example, George Kennan to Marshall, Paul Nitze to Acheson, and Robert Bowie and Gerard Smith to Dulles. Unfortunately, in recent years the planning function has been starved and ignored, which accounts in part for so much foreign policy being made in the White House and for its being so often conditioned by domestic politics.

In most respects the State Department needs to be much leaner and more flexible than it is. There are too many people in it, too many committees engaged in interminable incestuous confabulation, and too many clearances required before action can be taken. The population of the Department could usefully be cut 30 percent or more, of which the largest slice should come from the administrative side, since over the past twenty-five years whenever the managers have been asked to reorganize the Department they have begun, and often ended, by adding more of their own kind. Committees should be drastically reduced in numbers and size; ten members should be the maximum, five or six the optimum. If a memorandum or recommendation to the top or a telegram of instruction to the field has to have more than five initials, it will be a clear sign the Department has not yet been sufficiently streamlined.

These same principles of centralization of authority and delegation of responsibility, of leanness of figure and briskness of mind, should also apply to the organization and conduct of the Foreign Service, though due account has to be taken of the peculiar requirements of an institution scattered at four hundred and fifty posts throughout the world. Most officers should be recruited at the bottom, and the majority should expect to make it a lifetime career. However, there must be appropriate procedures for taking in a small number of outsiders at all levels to refresh the bureaucracy, and even to take in large numbers in some categories to meet special emergencies. At the same time there must be equally standard procedures for weeding out officers who experience reveals are unsuited to this kind of life or are not equipped to fill senior positions. This process should be most rigorous during the first five years, but it must continue throughout the career at all levels if deadwood is to be prevented from accumulating at the top. These procedures should be accompanied and balanced by a promotion system which rapidly rewards unusual ability and initiative, regularly invigorates the middle and upper echelons with younger persons and conspicuously provides a "career open to talents."

There is a perennial argument in foreign and other services as to the relative merits or proper balance between specialists and generalists. In my judgment, the broader a man's knowledge, interests and sympathies are, the more likely he is to be perceptive and successful in every field of action, including foreign affairs. An officer who knows something of history, science, sociology, psychology and religion, as well as the more conventional skills of diplomacy, will better understand and cope with governments and people of any country, including his own. Even though they may have started as specialists, it is almost invariably men who have become generalists who rise to the top.

At the same time specialists are obviously needed, more in these days than in the past. It is impossible to know a great deal about everything. It is advantageous to have both trained political scientists and trained economists —as long as they are fully aware their learning will never be truly "scientific" in the sense that of natural scientists can be. It is advantageous to have men and women who have spent years schooling themselves in the customs, psychology and language of a particular culture—as long as they do not so fall in love with the culture that they lose all objectivity in regard to it or do not fix their attention so exclusively on it that they forget the rest of the world.

Lastly, a word about the role and selection of ambassadors. There is a misconception that in the world of modern communications the ambassador is so close to Washington, so much under its thumb, that he is little more than a messenger boy, or at best a ceremonial figure.

This is far from being the truth. He remains the representative and spokesman of the President and the Secretary of State to the government to which he is accredited. On him and his embassy will depend in large measure whether or not Washington has an accurate understanding of what is happening and is likely to happen in that country. His reporting and that of his embassy will go far toward determining the attitude of the President and the Secretary toward the government of the country, and his recommendations will strongly influence our policy toward that country. He is the exponent and advocate of U.S. policy in his post, and on him and his embassy will greatly depend whether the government and people of the country will correctly understand and judge (whether or not they agree with) that policy.

There also rests with the ambassador the primary responsibility for holding together in a disciplined and harmonious body all the disparate elements of his embassy despatched by many different U.S. agencies, and for ensuring that all of them report in a coordinated fashion to Washington and speak with a single voice to the government and people of the host country. Few tasks of an ambassador have been more ungrateful and onerous since World War II, despite any number of Presidential orders over the years giving him the widest authority in these respects. A major cause is that the various agencies are still not adequately coordinated and subordinated in Washington; another is that the personnel of many of them in the field is so superabundant and superfluous that a large proportion of them can keep busy only by doing what others are doing or what should not be done at all.

In any case, men and women with such extensive and critical responsibilities as those of an ambassador should be chosen with the utmost care. It is as outrageous and irresponsible to select for such positions inexperienced and unqualified people, solely on the ground of their financial or other contributions to a political party, as it would be to select generals, admirals or astronauts on the same grounds. This practice was tolerable for the isolated and parochial United States of the nineteenth century; it is intolerable for a nation that is involved throughout the world and often presumes to lead it.

In 1972 more than a third of our ambassadors were still political appointees, and only three embassies in Western Europe, the area of greatest concentration of our national interest, were headed by career diplomats. Our ambassadors to Japan, India, Pakistan, Canada, Australia and New Zealand were also political appointees. No other great power, and very few small ones, behave so foolishly. It would be one thing to reserve 5 percent of our embassies for such outstanding and eminently qualified public figures as Harriman, Bruce, Lodge, Dillon and Bunker. It is quite another to reserve more than 30 percent, including most of the most critical, for amateurs wholly without diplomatic training or experience.

Finally, it is often said that, unlike the Defense, Commerce, Labor and Agriculture Departments, the State Department has no constituency among the American people and therefore lacks the necessary support for its policies and budgets among the Congress and the public. If this is so, it is the State Department's fault. If it is to be, as it should be, the department of government whose responsibility it is to harmonize our relations with the rest of the world and to keep us out of war and trouble, it has an enormous natural constituency which it needs only to cultivate. It should have in that constituency most of the millions of church members or at least churchgoers of the country; it should have most of the millions of young men and women who want to live out their time; it should have the millions of those citizens, still impoverished, whose best hope of rising out of poverty lies in a reordering of national priorities; it should have the millions of men and women of intelligence and goodwill who are aware that a more stable world order is essential to the survival of everyone. In order to rally these constituencies behind it, however, the Department needs to take a leaf out of the Pentagon's book and devote far more time and energy than it has to informing them, to listening to them and to establishing a permanent country-wide network of community relations.

The Defense Department   Since an earlier section of this book has dealt at length with the involvement of the military in foreign affairs, it will not be necessary to say much at this point about the place of the Pentagon and its representatives abroad in the foreign-affairs apparatus.

Obviously in a world as troubled and as dangerous as ours, the Defense Department has a legitimate—indeed, an indispensable—part to play in this structure. I well remember that in the years immediately preceding World War II, particularly after the Japanese invasion of China in 1937, liaison among the State, War and Navy Departments was constant and intimate. It was also a time, however, when, though President Roosevelt's regard for most of the people in his State Department was meager, the military services also occupied a modest place in the hierarchy of national decision-making. The problem now is how, after the military has for three decades bestrode "the narrow world like a Colossus," to contract its scope and power in the determination of foreign policy, without infringing upon its proper prerogatives in the formulation of military policy and requirements.

The military's most elevated involvement and its normal access to the President will no doubt continue to be through the participation of the Secretary of Defense and the Chairman of the Joint Chiefs of Staff in the National Security Council, the purpose of which, it is worth recalling again, was to give President Truman "a perpetual inventory of where we stood and where we were going on all strategic questions affecting the national security."

This is a broad mandate and should give the Defense Department through its membership in the NSC opportunity at the highest level to express its views on foreign policies affecting the national defense. It should *not* permit the Secretary of Defense and the Joint Chiefs of Staff to usurp the role of the Secretary of State by insisting on "strategic" decisions in the Western Pacific, Southeast Asia, the Indian Ocean, the Mediterranean or the Azores, which determine and distort foreign policy. General Taylor and Secretary McNamara had more to do with involving us too deeply in Vietnam than did Secretary Rusk.

Beneath the NSC, liaison between the State and Defense Departments should be extremely close at all levels, as indeed it often is. The Secretary of State should lunch once a week with the Secretary of Defense. Other officers of the State Department should be in regular and frequent contact with the Undersecretary of Defense, the Joint Chiefs and their Joint Staff, the Assistant Secretary for International Security Affairs, and the Defense intelligence agencies. This whole apparatus of consultation should be within the context of the overriding authority of the Secretary of State in regard to foreign affairs; that is, it should be for the purpose of assuring that military operations and planning conform to established foreign policy rather than of assuring that foreign policy conforms to recommended defense requirements.

As to overseas representation, the military are almost always the worst offenders in overstaffing U.S. embassies and missions abroad. Mention has already been made of the Military Assistance Advisory Groups, which are intended to administer military aid to foreign countries. It can almost be stated as an axiom that as military aid expands by arithmetical progression, these groups expand by geometrical progression, usually out of all proportion to real needs and often causing overinvolvement in both military and political affairs of the recipient countries.

Somewhat less dangerous in their implications but even less justifiable on grounds of actual need are the vastly inflated staffs of the service (that is, military intelligence) attachés assigned to U.S. embassies. Though the work they perform at many posts is trivial and could be carried out by two or three persons, they are often more numerous and usually better housed and supported than their civilian counterparts. Three-quarters of them are superfluous and should be sent promptly home.

If I may be permitted an obiter dictum, the real problem is that the U.S. military officer corps is far larger than it need or should be. It was enormously expanded during World War II, was maintained and elaborated for NATO, the Cold War, Korea and Vietnam, and has successfully resisted the demobilization which followed every other war in our history. The situation is aggravated by the competition and duplication involved in having three independent Services, one of which, in my heretical opinion, the Air Force, should never have been separated from the Army. In any case, when one steadily brings into an elite corps, such as these three, a larger number of able and ambitious young men than can in fact be usefully employed in any circumstances short of World War III, several consequences inevitably follow. Since sufficient interesting and prestigious jobs do not exist, they have to be invented. A substantial number of these unnecessary jobs are inserted in the foreign-affairs apparatus, primarily abroad, because these are at the least glamorous and comfortable, and at best partially authentic. Even if a job is not necessary, an able and conscientious officer will want to make it so by building it up with all the Yankee ingenuity and drive he can muster. When thousands of conscientious American military officers in scores of foreign countries busy themselves in this fashion, the unsought and unforeseen consequences for our national security can be quite appalling. The situation is essentially uncontrollable either by the State Department, the

Defense Department or U.S. ambassadors, as long as the number of ambitious and underemployed officers is so vast. The only solution would seem to be to shrink their numbers drastically.

The Central Intelligence Agency

How important in modern international affairs is intelligence, and how essential is secrecy? In my view "intelligence"—that is, information—is extremely important, but except in regard to the technology and deployment of weapons, it can be acquired with modest diligence and without an elaborate covert apparatus. Most significant current "intelligence" is published in the daily, weekly or monthly press. The principal difficulty is not too little information but too much. If there is an "information overload" on the average citizen, who is exposed to the factitious agitation of "news" on the air every hour of the day and night, how much more of an overload is there on the policy-maker in government who is inundated almost from minute to minute by reports, cables, "flashes" and phone calls from all over the world? The real difficulty is to distinguish fact from fancy, the significant from the trivial, the constant from the ephemeral.

These needs can usually be supplied in international affairs by three complementary networks: a network of embassies abroad staffed by officers intimately acquainted with the people, personalities and problems of their area of assignment; a much smaller network of analytical and evaluating officers in Washington staffed by men and women equally experienced in the various geographic and functional areas; and a network of private research institutes whose work is independent but available to government.

What then is the utility of having, abroad and at home, an additional vast intelligence apparatus operating theoretically under cover, even though much of that cover is transparent? I think, very little, except in the weapons field. This does not mean that much proficient and useful political contact and reporting is not done by the Central Intelligence Agency; on the contrary. I have myself been the grateful recipient of enormous help from outstanding officers of this Agency over the past quarter century while I was chief or deputy chief of mission in Bangkok, Prague, Vienna, Athens, Vientiane, Paris and Rabat. But the fact is that nine-tenths of the really valuable contacts they have maintained and information they have collected could have been handled as well by State Department political officers if the embassies had been properly staffed for that purpose. In addition, this could have been done without the stigma and risks which attach to a covert operation and which reflect on the embassy sheltering such operations.

There remains the 10 percent or so of desirable political intelligence which cannot be collected by overt means, but this could either be garnered by vastly smaller covert stations than now exist or could be dispensed with altogether without great loss. The truly vital target for covert intelligence these days is the technology and deployment of weapons. Most of this is now collected by sophisticated electronic devices, immensely costly and requiring substantial numbers of designers, operators and analysts, but this is a far cry from political intelligence and the conduct of foreign affairs.

One more aspect of intelligence collection, though it is not a responsibility of the CIA, deserves brief mention: the interception of other governments' communications. In wartime this facility can be of the highest importance. It is well known that U.S. access to Japanese codes played a substantial part in our victory at Midway. On the other hand, judging by my reading of thousands of political intercepts from 1943 until my retirement in 1971, I am not convinced that the product obtained is significant enough to justify in peacetime the time, energy and funds expended. No doubt if one were able to read the minutes of the Politburo, the exercise might be worth the cost, but it seems unlikely that interception will ever be that cunning. Most of what *is* available emanates from less sophisticated governments, and 99 percent of it could be known or deduced from more legitimate sources. Despite the alibi of "national interest" and the fascination of cryptography, I have never felt entirely comfortable reading other people's mail—particularly when so much of it is so trivial and dull.

A major aspect of the CIA's work is the analysis and assessment of the enormous quantities of "raw" intelligence received. A large part of this soggy mass could be better evaluated at embassies on the spot and eliminated without being sent to headquarters. The question remains whether what political and economic information is sent needs to be analyzed and evaluated at two places in Washington—the State Department and the CIA. It is argued that this competition or duplication keeps both on their toes, prevents either from being too complacent or overconfident and offers the President a range of judgments rather than a single prefabricated one. I am not persuaded by these arguments. One can imagine the consequences if we had two weather bureaus, each issuing separate and competing forecasts; one is quite confusing enough. How is a President equipped to judge between two contradictory judgments or forecasts about a development in, say, Afghanistan?

I favor the centralization in the State Department of research and analysis on foreign affairs, with the stipulation that whenever there is a sharp difference of opinion among the analysts on an important matter, this difference not be papered over but be reported candidly to the Secretary and the President. Healthy competition among experts is quite as feasible within a single properly managed organization as between two duplicating ones. After all, ample competition is offered by the press in a democracy. Indeed, whether there are one or five government agencies involved, they and their judgments are all too likely to conform, consciously or unconsciously, to the official line. The shrewder journalists were right about Vietnam far more often than the CIA, State, Defense and the White House together, despite the profusion of intelligence theoretically available to the latter. The lesson may be that one man with an open mind is worth a thousand with an obsession or a predisposition.

What about covert operations, the so-called department of "dirty tricks" which James Bond has so endearingly portrayed for us? These have already diminished considerably since their heyday in the 1950's and the monumental fiasco at the Bay of Pigs. Their success was never as great as was claimed, for example, in Iran or Guatemala, where indigenous forces played the decisive role. On the other hand, notoriety at home was skillfully avoided for such egregious blunders as the Syrian "coup" of 1957, the Lebanese "election" that brought on the civil war in 1958, and the intrusion into Laotian politics which produced the "neutralist" revolt of 1960 and the occupation of half the country by the North Vietnamese. Ham-handed hanky-panky ruined the reputation of the CIA in many Third World countries already sensitive to intervention in their affairs and to covert attempts to manipulate or subvert them. The salient fact about such operations is not so much that they are sinful as that they are self-defeating. Even if at first they seem to succeed, they often stimulate antibodies which ultimately destroy them. While I would not go so far as to exclude covert operations altogether, as long as we confront such nasty practitioners as the Soviets, I am convinced that they should be resorted to most sparingly and only after the most careful appraisal of pros and cons by senior officials in Washington.

It is only fair to conclude these disparaging remarks by noting that most of the faults in covert operations and intelligence here attributed to the CIA and other U.S.

agencies are conscious imitations—often pale in comparison—of Soviet behavior and practice. It is melancholy to reflect that the political system established by Lenin to free the downtrodden and unite the workers of the world has created the most colossal, unscrupulous and vicious police apparatus in history—an apparatus which swept away most of the Soviet elite in the 1930's and most of the East European elite in the forties, fifties and sixties, which continues to tyrannize triumphantly over the whole Soviet empire, and which has infected most of the rest of the world with an unholy legion of spies, bullies and fifth columnists. What is perhaps even sadder is the extent to which those outside the empire have found it expedient to copy some of its most unattractive practices in the realm of espionage and counterespionage—indeed, in many ways to become a mirror image of what they are resisting. It is claimed that it is necessary to fight fire with fire, but I have always found water more helpful. To put it in old-fashioned terms, it has usually seemed to me both more righteous and more profitable to expose evil than to match it.

The Agency for International Development, the Treasury, Commerce, Labor and Agriculture Departments, and the U.S. Information Service   Ever since the inception of the Marshall Plan in 1947 there have been agencies in Washington and missions throughout the world to administer U.S. economic-aid programs. Sometimes these agencies have been under the administrative control of the State Department, at others only under its policy direction. The missions abroad have almost always been attached, sometimes closely, sometimes loosely, to U.S. embassies, and their directors have been important members of the "country teams" under the ambassador.

Obviously, the ability to grant or withhold vast sums of

money has added a new dimension to the conduct of U.S. foreign policy. Not surprisingly, the largest amounts have been bestowed on those countries either allied with us or especially exposed to Communist attack or pressure. However, substantial amounts at one time or another have been made available to a majority of the world's non-Communist nations, in many cases disinterestedly to assist in development or to prevent suffering, in others to preserve the friendship of a strategically placed government and to keep it in power, in still others to forestall or compete with Communist aid programs.

Even in places where the aim has been almost entirely relief or development, sound business practice and Congressional pressure have required close supervision of our aid programs. In countries where the objectives are primarily political, this supervision involves not only a constant endeavor, often in vain, to ensure that the aid is in fact used to build broad public support for the recipient government, but also a concern with local politics which almost inevitably draws the American embassy and aid mission into the struggle between ins and outs. Because of the fact that U.S. aid has come to constitute a major part of the national income and national budget in many countries, American officials have held in their hands the life and death of governments. This power is resented by the local politicians and elite, but is for the most part tolerated as long as the aid is indispensable, or as long as it substantially profits the groups that receive and manipulate it.

On the whole, foreign-aid administrators and directors at home and abroad have not attempted to usurp the role of foreign-policy-makers and have worked in harmonious and mutually respectful partnership with the State Department and its ambassadors. There have been occasions when an aid administrator in Washington with White House support has ignored the Secretary of State. There have been times when an aid director, more able or more ambitious than his ambassador, has taken advantage of the influence which his bulging purse gives him with the local government to determine U.S. policy toward that country in important respects. These anomalies, however, have been rare, and with the recent sharp decline in our bilateral aid programs they should become rarer. Nevertheless, there are still significant problems of coordination in this area. Before defining them, however, the other U.S. agencies involved should be mentioned.

Rightly or wrongly, since World War I, several of the traditional U.S. government departments have made good a claim to play a significant part in the conduct of foreign affairs. The Treasury Department has an obvious and legitimate interest in international monetary matters, and on these often deals directly with foreign governments, either through the International Monetary Fund and other international institutions, or bilaterally through Treasury attachés in embassies abroad. Sometimes, however, Secretaries of the Treasury are not content with this substantial role. During World War II Henry Morgenthau concerned himself with the future of Germany and worked for its fragmentation and "pastoralization." During the last six months of 1971 it almost seemed that John Connally was conducting the foreign affairs of the United States, explicitly with the other developed countries, indirectly with much of the rest of the world.

The Departments of Commerce, Agriculture and Labor have also long concerned themselves intimately with the conduct of foreign affairs. From time to time the first two have had separate foreign services designed to maximize the export of American manufactured and farm products. Secretaries of Commerce and Agriculture frequently combine junkets overseas with the role of traveling salesmen. The Labor Department has a network of labor attachés in our embassies and through them maintains often politically significant ties with labor movements in many countries. Incidentally, the AFL-CIO also conducts its own foreign relations parallel to but not identical with those of the Labor Department. The foreign operations of each of these departments are encouraged and protected by the Congressional committees that watch over them, ostensibly on the grounds that the State Department does not sufficiently support these special American interests overseas, but also because the glamour of foreign affairs induces all who can fabricate an excuse to get into the act.

In any case, when a massively funded aid administration and four major government departments are directly involved in the formulation of foreign economic policy and the conduct of foreign economic affairs, horrendous and unresolved problems of coordination are created, particularly in Washington but also overseas. In some respects the central problem is not dissimilar to that of politico-military affairs, which has been met in the Nixon Administration by attributing sweeping responsibilities to the National Security Council and its staff in the White House. In a similar fashion, in 1971 the White House set up a Council on International Economic Policy, in which the heads of all the above-mentioned departments, as well as the ubiquitous National Security Adviser, are represented.

I have some of the same reservations about this Council as I have about the NSC. It is not essential to effective decision-making by the President that the apparatus for formulating the issues, examining the possible choices and making appropriate recommendations be located in the White House. The whole structure of government is subverted if the traditional departments are drained of authority, and duplicating bureaucracies screened from Congressional and public scrutiny are set up under the shadow of the President. It is true that a considerable number of executive departments are involved and have in the past been poorly coordinated. For example, our delegates at international conferences too often represent the interests of separate departments and interest groups rather than the foreign policy of the United States. On the other hand, there is no essential reason why those departments primarily charged with domestic responsibilities should be so deeply involved in the conduct of foreign affairs as they have come to be. The more agencies are involved the more unavoidable are compromises, and therefore the less clear, coherent and effective the policies are likely to be. If they contain something for each one, they may add up to nothing for everyone.

My own belief is that the conduct of international economic affairs, like that of other foreign affairs, is most simply and effectively handled if it is delegated by the President to the Secretary of State, and by him to an Undersecretary for Economic Affairs with wide authority to supervise and coordinate the limited activities of other departments and agencies in this field. One recalls the outstanding fashion in which this latter office has been filled in the past by such men as Will Clayton, Douglas Dillon and George Ball. There may still be need for a council of department and agency heads under the chairmanship of the President, whose task would be to discuss and determine the broad lines of foreign economic policy, but it should be serviced and its decisions implemented by the Undersecretary of State and his staff, rather than by an independent executive director and staff in the White House. There is also little need for separate representation overseas for other departments and agencies in the economic field, except for those carrying out economic aid and development programs; the overseas representatives of these, like those of the military and the CIA, should be unequivocally placed under the authority of the ambassador.

One other government agency involved in the conduct of foreign affairs needs to be briefly mentioned. The U.S. Information Service has at times been attached to the State Department and at times has been separate. Its purpose is to disseminate overseas—particularly in countries lacking either the will or the means to extend full freedom of information—American policy and opinion. Its instruments for doing so include the Voice of America, broadcasting daily in thirty-five languages, and a staff at most of our embassies which maintains libraries, distributes publications and cultivates press and opinion leaders.

A government agency in this field faces the insoluble dilemma of either hewing strictly to the official line and thereby losing credibility with much of its foreign audience, or of reflecting the wide diversity of behavior and opinion in the United States and thus constantly incurring the wrath of the White House, State Department and Congress. The chief consequence of this dilemma has been that over a period of twenty-five years the agency has been repeatedly expanded and contracted like an accordion, with disastrous effects on its morale and effectiveness. My personal experience has been that on the whole it has done a very good job under these trying circumstances, and I believe that its principal activities are worth preserving. It must, however, be given sufficient latitude to reflect what the United States *really* is, and not what its leaders would like it to appear to be, if the agency is to keep both the attention and confidence of the foreign audiences to which it addresses itself.

The Congress   The formal role of the Congress in the conduct of foreign affairs is confined to three functions: declarations of war or national emergencies; advice and consent by the Senate to treaties and to nomination of senior officials; approval of funds for the support of the departments concerned and of foreign-aid programs. When these functions are conservatively interpreted by the Congress and when the administration is careful to work closely with Congressional leaders concerned with foreign affairs, the system works reasonably well. But in recent years neither of these conditions has been met, and consequently there has developed a persistent feud between the executive and legislative branches which has not been conducive to the felicitous conduct of foreign affairs.

The fault lies primarily with the last three administrations, which involved the country in a major war and carried it on for years without the explicit advice and consent of Congress; which concealed or manipulated facts in order to obtain Congressional approval for huge appropriations for this war; and which permitted the military-industrial complex to make critical and often foolish decisions in regard to a vast and unnecessary expansion of our arsenal of weapons.

To be sure, members of Congress are not children and cannot plausibly disavow their own responsibility for approving year after year—indeed, up until the present—the funds on which these actions and programs depended. The fact is that while a growing minority in Congress has been radically changing their views on these matters since about 1968, a majority continues to share with the Executive the conventional wisdom which lured us into war in Indochina and compulsive military competition with the Soviet Union. However, the growing minority has become sufficiently stubborn and powerful to complicate seriously the conduct of foreign affairs by the last two administrations. Indeed in its frustrated zeal to correct tragic errors and recapture its constitutional authority it has occasionally seemed to want the United States to resign from the world.

The first step toward reestablishing a healthy collaboration between the executive and legislative branches on foreign affairs would be for the former to consult more closely and candidly with the appropriate leaders of the Senate and House, and to determine henceforth to make no significant move or new departure without a frank prior explanation to these leaders of its rationale. However, even this more intimate and consistent consultation will not be enough. The President must not only listen to, but must heed, the views on foreign policy of Congressional leaders, even when these differ radically from his own. Such open-mindedness will not be easy in a time of transition when there is indiscriminate popular revulsion against old policies but as yet no consensus as to which of them may be still relevant and necessary and which outmoded and dispensable. Still, the effort must be made quickly, honestly and persistently if present deadlock and drift are to be overcome before they do grave damage to our national interests and authority.

If the Executive proves unwilling to permit a more meaningful participation of the Congress in the formulation of policy, the Congress will have no alternative but to exercise a far more rigorous control over the purse strings, drastically curtailing military and economic programs which have not been justified rather than merely nibbling away at their edges. But more genuine participation by the Congress in foreign-policy-making places on it a greater responsibility itself to eschew extreme shifts of emotion and interest. Because there has been too much military aid, it does not follow that suddenly there should be none. Because economic aid has contributed in some cases to inordinate U.S. involvement in dangerous situations does not mean that economic aid in general should be drastically reduced; perhaps in the broad perspective of the future it needs to be drastically increased. Because the U.S. domestic economy has suffered a recession and a fall in productivity does not mean that we should succumb again to a misleading "protectionism" which contributed so much to the Great Depression of the 1930's.

If the Congress expects to play a greater and more constructive role in the formulation and guidance of foreign policy, there is also one respect, by no means peculiar to foreign affairs, in which it must put its own house in order. This is the inordinate authority and discretion accorded to committee and subcommittee chairmen. James MacGregor Burns has recently written: "If an analyst were ever able to uncover the prime *institutional* reason for the lagging social progress of the 1950's and the upheavals of the 1960's, surely it would be the structure of negativism built into both houses [of Congress]."*

This structure applies equally and cogently to significant aspects of the Congressional role in the conduct of foreign affairs. For example, out of a perverted sense of status or courtesy, narrow-minded and capricious subcommittee chairmen, such as John Rooney of Brooklyn or Otto Passman of Louisiana, are permitted year after year after year to wield dictatorial power over the budget of the State Department or the shape of the foreign-aid program. The tangible and intangible damage these two men and others like them have done over the past two decades to the effective conduct of U.S. foreign policy, not to mention harmonious collaboration between the executive and legislative branches, is incalculable. On the other hand, the vast majority of the members of the Senate Foreign Relations Committee and the House Foreign Affairs Committee have in recent years been men of breadth, dedication and impartiality, and their role in foreign affairs, though narrowly restricted by succeeding administrations, has been significant and constructive.

The Intellectual Establishment

In the United States there exists, between government departments and agencies concerned with foreign affairs and private organizations, institutes, foundations and

---

*James MacGregor Burns, *Uncommon Sense* (New York: Harper & Row, 1972).

"think tanks" similarly concerned, a symbiotic relationship which is unique in degree and of great advantage to both.

The faculty and research fellows of history and political-science departments and schools of international affairs at such great universities as Harvard, Columbia, Princeton, Stanford, Chicago and MIT, the staff of research institutes (for example, Brookings and Rand), the staff and members of such organizations as the Council on Foreign Relations, the Carnegie Endowment, the United Nations Association, the Foreign Policy Association, and the staff of great foundations (Ford, Rockefeller and others)—all of these constitute a constituency, a supplementary research and analysis resource, and a reservoir of talent for the State Department and related agencies. The so-called "in-and-outer," the expert in one or another field of foreign affairs who moves back and forth from government to private university or institute, carries, by a sort of alternating current, refreshment and new ideas to the bureaucracy, and pragmatism to the think tank or school, with substantial profit to both and to himself. No other country so regularly and easily avails itself of this resource.

It is important, however, to note one serious peril in this process. If an outsider without practical experience in foreign affairs, even though he may have vast "scientific" erudition and outstanding intellectual ability, is suddenly placed in an exalted position in government, such as that of National Security Adviser to the President, he may be tempted to try to carry out dogmatically some of the elegant but theoretical conceptions he has distilled in his ivory tower and elaborated in his books. This intellectual hubris, untested by sufficient exposure to the harsh realities of the world outside the United States, may cause grave injury to his country and to himself. Therefore, my recommendation would be that the valuable "in-and-outer" from academic life be employed widely in the middle ranks of the government foreign-affairs apparatus, but that he be permitted to rise to the top only if and when extensive practical experience has calibrated his grasp with his reach.

Another fruitful aspect of the symbiotic relationship between the public and private foreign-affairs establishments is the way in which the former, harassed and preoccupied by the pressure of day-to-day business and crisis, relies on the latter for a steady injection of fresh ideas, more careful research and longer-range perspective. Concurrently this interaction, working through universities and associations having a wide popular membership, helps create in the electorate a foreign-affairs constituency which both provides indispensable public support for foreign policies and serves as a pressure group acting on government to correct policies which the private establishment perceives have lost their heavenly mandate. Thus, foreign policy, which traditionally in all countries —and still too often in some—was the private preserve of a narrow elite, is anchored firmly in the most politically alert and active part of the electorate.

For this reason it is both depressing and exasperating to find some of the most idealistic younger members of university faculties, and many of their students, self-righteously insisting that their schools or universities have no truck at all with the wicked government, particularly with the State and Defense Departments and the CIA because they disapprove of the Vietnam war or other ugly aspects of current foreign relations. By so doing they deny themselves and their schools the best possible access to government and the best means of influencing it steadily and democratically along lines they favor. Similarly, they deny themselves relevant participation in this critical arena of the world outside their cloistered halls—a relevance and a participation they clamor for whenever it is not offered. But this is probably a passing phase. The glamour, drama and ever more intimate impact of foreign affairs will soon lead the bees back to the honey and revive the fertile conjugation of those who act without time to think and those who think without occasion to act.

The News Media   It would be derogatory and misleading to conclude this survey of the instruments involved in the management and mismanagement of American foreign affairs without a brief mention of the news media. Particularly in an area of government where the Executive is so predominant, where it is so intermittently responsive to Congress and public opinion, and where its weakness for secrecy is so easily carried to ridiculous extremes, the role of the news media in informing, alerting and inciting public opinion is absolutely critical.

All Presidents and some Vice-Presidents complain bitterly about this role of a free press, but the electorate should only complain that there is not enough of it. Aside from a few large metropolitan journals, most newspapers contain shockingly little news of foreign affairs and even less intelligent analysis. Television treatment of foreign events is extensive but too often superficial, zooming in on the melodramatic or the trivial for a brief moment between commercials in a way that often confuses more than it enlightens. Still, the persistent visual impact either of melodrama or of triviality produces over the long run some unexpected effects; war, for instance, is less romantic when it drips blood every night in the parlor or bedroom.

It seems pertinent to these remarks about the news media to say a few words about official secrecy and classification of government documents, which has become such a hotly contested issue since the publication of the Pentagon and Anderson Papers. For years there has been an enormous exaggeration of the need for secrecy in the conduct of international affairs. Seventy percent of the political and economic information which is classified confidential or secret, much even that is classified top secret or higher, could be published without serious benefit to foreign governments or more than temporary embarrassment to our own.

Classified political information consists for the most part of "intelligence" reports and evaluation; conversations with foreign governments and individuals; our own policies, either approved or under consideration; and positions we intend to put forward in negotiations. What governments feel the most need to conceal are their sources (who said what about whom); extreme policies considered but discarded; how much one knows or suspects about an adversary's plans; and fallback positions for later stages of a negotiation. There are sound and obvious reasons for withholding the first two of these indefinitely. There are also good reasons for withholding the last two temporarily, though if they leak out it is rare that national security is endangered. What is likely to be lost is negotiating flexibility, as all those who have ever sought "open covenants openly arrived at" have discovered. Once a negotiating position has been revealed to the public, even if it was put forward only for bargaining purposes, it becomes much more difficult to back away from it, even if to do so would result in an agreement strongly in the national interest.

However, it is far more vital to ensure that public opinion understands, approves and will support what is being sought. To this end, wide public information is essential, and if that information is too selective, its bias and inaccuracy will sooner or later emerge and erode its credibility. What is needed in this respect, therefore, is a radical shift in emphasis. Governments have tended to publish only what could not conceivably be damaging; they need in fact to conceal only what could unquestionably be dangerous. Even more critical, the criterion should be that it is dangerous to national security strictly defined, rather than dangerous to the domestic political image a President is trying to create.

I would therefore recommend a large decrease in the number of documents which are classified at all, a substantial decrease in those which are highly classified and, most important of all, a consistent policy of informing the Congress and the public much more fully and frankly what the government knows or believes, what its real objectives are, what it proposes to do and how, and what it proposes *not* to do and why.

Therefore, with certain obvious exceptions, which honorable gentlemen and gentlewomen of the press will respect, the more they can pry loose from coy politicians and bureaucrats about the conduct of foreign affairs, the better they will be serving their country. But what is most needed from them is not the latest piece of hot news, which any fool can dig up and report, but objective considered judgment about the significance and motivation of what is doing and what is brewing behind the scenes at home and abroad. The public needs not to be shocked but to be forewarned.

Summary and   On the basis of this examina-
Conclusions   tion of the management of
                     foreign affairs in the United
                     States, I wish to emphasize
six requirements which should be met, with far more firmness and sophistication than they have been, if the *mis*management which has so often characterized our performance during recent years is to be avoided. These requirements apply whether the United States remains as deeply and obtrusively involved in global affairs as it has been since World War II, or whether it adopts a "lower profile," retreats into relative isolation or more consistently relies on multilateral institutions.

In my view, the first requirement is for an organization which serves but does not encumber the President; which fixes authority and responsibility at the Cabinet level; which provides machinery for bringing to its decision-makers major issues and essential information (but not minor information and trivial information); which ensures insofar as possible that decisions will be taken with "all deliberate speed" in the light of available and relevant intelligence and expertise; and which ensures a faithful and coordinated implementation of decisions in Washington and overseas.

This requirement cannot be met in these times by a President acting alone in the style of Wilson or Roosevelt, nor by prestigious advisers and large staffs in the White House duplicating and confusing the responsibilities of the senior Cabinet officer and his department. On the contrary, the requirement could be best applied if the President were to confer on the Secretary of State unequivocal authority and responsibility, under the Chief Executive, for the conduct of foreign affairs. The Department of State and its ambassadors would work in closest cooperation with other departments and agencies having a valid interest in aspects of foreign affairs, but, subject to appeal to the President, the decisions of the Secretary of State as to the confines of his authority would be final. For this system to be effective, the President and the Secretary would have to work in the most harmonious intimacy, and the former would have to support consistently the authority of the latter in the inevitable and perennial attacks against it and evasions of it.

Secondly, the same requirement of central authority and sound organization would have to obtain inside the State Department and in its relations with other agencies. Decision-making on major issues would be the responsibility of a group of about ten senior officers, with decision-making on lesser issues decentralized throughout the Department and among ambassadors abroad. It would emphasize rapidity of action, small streamlined committees (where committees are necessary), a minimum of clearances and a relentless follow-up on issues pending and decisions taken.

The third requirement would be for a staffing of the senior echelons involved, in and out of the State Department, by a judicious mixture of experienced nonprofessionals enjoying the particular confidence of the President and the Secretary, outstanding professionals with a lifetime of training in foreign affairs, and "in-and-outers" from the academic or business world with special expertise in certain relevant fields. Examples of the first category are Dean Acheson (as Assistant Secretary and Undersecretary), Adolph Berle, William Benton, Robert Lovett, Averell Harriman, Paul Hoffman, Philip Jessup, Paul Nitze, David Bruce, Walter Bedell Smith, Christian Herter (as Undersecretary), Chester Bowles, George Ball and Elliot Richardson. Examples of the second category are Sumner Welles, George Kennan, Charles Bohlen, Walton Butterworth, Robert Murphy, Loy Henderson, Livingston Merchant, George Allen, Llewellyn Thompson, Foy Kohler, Joseph Sisco and Marshall Green. Examples of the third category are George Perkins, Robert Bowie, Gerard Smith, McGeorge Bundy, Harlan Cleveland, Walt Rostow, Roger Hilsman, Henry Kissinger and Peter Peterson. In regard to the third category, however, I would not recommend, in view of their lack of prior practical experience in the conduct of foreign affairs, that any such men initially occupy a position higher than Assistant Secretary of State, though after two or three years in such a position, no doubt many of them would qualify for higher responsibilities.

One more category of people, outside of the regular hierarchy, whose advice Presidents and Secretaries of State might seek at intervals, would be "elder statesmen." In addition to the obvious qualification of long experience, they have two others of even more critical importance. First, being outside those circles of government where an inward-oriented and self-serving climate of opinion tends to grow up and to warp judgment, they can, like men striding through a ground fog, look above and beyond it and tell the President what they see. Second, because they are not beholden to the President and have no favors to ask or expect of him, they can render him the service he needs most—that is, tell him the unpleasant truths running counter to his preconceived notions or political interests, with which his subordinates in government either do not want or do not dare to confront him. On the other hand, unless they are among those rare ones perennially young in spirit, men such as Averell Harriman or Paul Hoffman, elder statesmen should not be brought back into government itself, lest they apply indiscriminately to the unfamiliar present those doctrines and formulas they espoused in the more comprehensible past.

The fourth requirement to avoid mismanagement of foreign affairs is the efficient mobilization, integration, evaluation and application of intelligence in its widest sense. This means acquiring information through the official and unofficial networks described earlier, ensuring that these networks work in a complementary rather than a competitive fashion, that they report as much but no more than is necessary, that their product is analyzed and evaluated by trained specialists in the particular geographic and functional fields, and that it comes to the decision-makers in a form that excludes trivia but does not disguise dissent. This also means vastly reducing in size and scope the intelligence activities of the CIA and the Defense Department, and fixing more firmly the responsibility for analysis and evaluation of all intelligence collected in the State Department and Foreign Service.

Even more essential to successful policy is a high-level planning staff, locked intimately into the process of decision-making, through which the long-range implications of current events can be estimated, through which current policies can be continuously reexamined and reassessed, and through which plans for meeting future developments can be prepared and submitted to the high command. Theirs should be the task, day after day, year after year, of testing conceptual frameworks against pragmatic realities, of reconciling imperative consistencies with inevitable inconsistencies, of sternly examining and reexamining every aspect of the conventional wisdom, of adapting the doctrines of the past to the exigencies of the future. A foreign-policy apparatus without such a staff is a blind man groping and stumbling in the dark.

The fifth requirement is that drastic measures be taken to check the incidence of Parkinson's Law and the Peter Principle. This means sternly resisting the tendency common to all bureaucracies to multiply and proliferate their personnel, and to magnify their activities in order to occupy the superfluous manpower thus engendered. It also means having a personnel system hospitable to talent and inhospitable to mediocrity, so that the former moves more rapidly to the top and the latter does not float above its level of competence.

Since in both cases contrary processes have so long been the rule, what is first needed is a drastic shrinking of staffs at home and abroad. This would involve a reduction in force of the State Department of about one-third; a reduction in force of those parts of the CIA engaged in political and economic reporting and analysis and in covert operations of about three-quarters; a reduction in force of military-service attachés stationed abroad of at least three-quarters; reductions in force of other agencies commensurate with reductions of their function in foreign affairs discussed elsewhere. The reductions in State should be applied almost wholly in Washington, since Foreign Service field staffs of more or less present size may be required to take over the legitimate activities now being inappropriately performed by the CIA and other agencies.

If morale and achievement among the surviving streamlined staffs are to be preserved, such drastic reductions will obviously have to be carried out over a period of time, and with decent compensation for the innocent and generally able individuals affected. Moreover, in the State Department itself, where the preponderant share of responsibility for the conduct of foreign affairs should henceforth lie, care should be taken not to reduce further the modest annual recruitment at the bottom, lest the expectation among ambitious young people of a career consistently open to them in foreign affairs be too long disappointed and wither away.

The sixth and final requirement for avoiding mismanagement in our foreign affairs, which would hardly seem to need mention had it not been so grossly violated in recent times, is that the support of Congress and the public for the foreign policies of the administration be sought through candid, patient and painstaking explanation rather than by rhetoric, deception and *fait accompli.* For this purpose the most important first step—and in light of recent history it will not be an easy one—would be a revival of confidence between any administration and those leaders of the Senate and House most concerned with foreign affairs.

To this end, an administration would have to reform its conduct of such affairs in two major respects. It would need to drastically circumscribe its definition of secrecy, and it would need not only to explain its policies but to pay a decent respect to the opinions of those with whom it spoke. This could not and should not mean the transfer of the primary responsibility for the conduct of foreign affairs from the President and the Secretary of State to the Congress and the public. But it should mean a restoration of dialogue, of rapport and of mutual helpfulness which, if constructively practiced by both sides, could restore to U.S. foreign policy a solidity, consistency and respect at home and abroad which it has recently lost, to the grave detriment of our national interest.

The Use and Disuse
of International Institutions

The principal theme of the last part of this book is that only through a much more intensive use and development of international institutions in the future can the rational objects of foreign policy that modern technology demands be pursued with any hope of success. This section describes briefly the use and disuse of such institutions, chiefly the United Nations, in the recent past.

There can be little question that the United States provided the main inspiration and impetus for the creation of the United Nations. Without the genuine conviction and persistent initiative of Franklin Roosevelt, Cordell Hull and Edward Stettinius it would never have been born. The British took an active part, but it is doubtful that Churchill thought it would save the world. Indeed, he showed some doubt, quite rightly, that it would prove compatible with the British Empire. It is probable that Stalin considered it another Anglo-Saxon exercise in hypocrisy and flimflammery. Presumably he participated because his wartime allies attached such importance to it, because he did not want to be left out of something that could conceivably become significant as a theater of power politics, and because he wanted to be sure that it was not usable against the Soviet Union.

I was intimately associated with the United Nations, if not from the time of its conception at least from the time of its birth. At Dumbarton Oaks in 1944, where the basic draft of the Charter was hammered out by Americans, Russians and British, I took part in the drafting of the critical security sections, Chapters VI and VII. Oddly enough, the two individuals who played the largest part in this particular drafting were both of Russian birth. Leo Pasvolsky came to the United States as a boy and was at that time Special Assistant to Cordell Hull; Arkady Sobolev, from the Soviet Foreign Ministry, later became, first, an Undersecretary at the United Nations and, later, Soviet Permanent Representative there. Both men displayed an extraordinary combination of vision and practicality, and together they worked out in the drafts of those two chapters a system for the maintenance of international peace and security which could very well have achieved its purpose if the indispensable prerequisite—a modicum of cooperation between the United States and the Soviet Union—had been preserved.

I also attended the San Francisco Conference in 1945 as an assistant to its chairman, Secretary of State Edward R. Stettinius, Jr. The atmosphere at this conference was for the most part harmonious. In a bare two months the Charter was completed and signed by fifty states. Already, however, rifts in the cooperation among the great powers were beginning to appear and to be reflected in acrimonious arguments among Stettinius, Molotov and Eden. The two most significant related to Poland and Argentina. In case of the former, the Western powers believed that Stalin had broken the Yalta agreement about a fair balance between Communists and non-Communists in the Polish Provisional Government. In the latter, the Soviets believed that the Western leaders had broken the Yalta agreement specifying that only those nations which had declared war on the Axis (which Argentina under Peron had not) should be invited to be founding members of the United Nations.

These were the first of many bitter debates and confrontations during Stalin's lifetime in which the Cold War was reflected in the UN, distorting its purpose and crippling its operation. For this reason it was never possible to negotiate the agreements envisaged in Article 43 of the Charter by which the great powers and other states were to make available to the UN the necessary forces and facilities for checking threats and punishing breaches of the peace. Consequently the Soviet Union, whose adherents were always in a small minority in both the Security Council and the Assembly, felt called upon to use the veto with great frequency in defense of its interests and those of its friends. Thanks to the fortuitous absence of the Soviets from the Council in June 1950 the United States was able to use that body to mobilize resistance to the

Korean aggression, but this involvement plunged the UN even more deeply into the Cold War. As a further consequence, for twenty years the newly victorious Communist government of China was unwisely excluded from the United Nations, which was thereby for all that time deprived of the ability to represent accurately the real situation in East Asia.

After Stalin's death the effectiveness of the UN improved for a number of reasons. First, the Cold War somewhat abated. Second, an extremely able and vigorous Secretary General, Dag Hammarskjöld, was in office from 1953 to 1961. Third, there was a vast increase in membership, mostly from states in the Third World which needed both the protection of the UN against the great powers and against each other, and its assistance in their economic and social development. Fourth, in the absence of Article 43 agreements, Hammarskjöld and others worked out reasonably effective ad hoc procedures for UN peacekeeping which were successfully applied in the Middle East from 1957 to 1967, in the Congo from 1960 to 1964, in Cyprus from 1964 to the present, between India and Pakistan in 1965, and elsewhere in less substantial fashion. Fifth, the U.S. Presidents of this period—Truman, Eisenhower and Kennedy—were at least modestly disposed to foster and strengthen the United Nations. Sixth, even the Soviet Union came at least to acquiesce in some of the UN's peace-keeping and development activities which did not threaten Soviet interests and were strongly supported by Third World members. Finally, the UN agencies for assistance were greatly expanded and invigorated during these years, particularly the Development Program under Paul Hoffman, the World Bank under Eugene Black, George Woods and Robert McNamara, and later the various regional banks.

On the other hand, since 1964 the United Nations has suffered a series of setbacks which have substantially *reduced* its effectiveness. By far the most serious of these has been the decline in U.S. interest and support under Presidents Johnson and Nixon. The United Nations was originally designed by its American founders to achieve two complementary ends: to involve the U.S. in world affairs so thoroughly as to preclude a relapse into the isolationism of the interwar years; and to do so through practical machinery for "harmonizing the actions of nations," which would also preclude a relapse into the power politics of those times. To this end, from 1944 to 1964 the United States provided most of the political energy and financial lubrication which kept the UN growing.

Beginning in 1964, however, the United States itself relapsed into power politics and large-scale military action outside the framework of the United Nations. To be sure, there were efforts to bring the question of Vietnam before the United Nations, but only, it must be admitted, to obtain its blessing for what the United States was determined in any case to do unilaterally. When the UN membership proved unwilling to act in our support—indeed, was in large part highly critical of us—Washington called the organization impotent and irresponsible.

U.S. support for the UN was also diminished when the Soviet Union and France refused to pay their assessed share of the expenses of the Congo operation, and when the majority of the membership refused to invoke Article 19 of the Charter to deprive those two states of their vote in the Assembly. The United States paid little heed to the rebuttal of friendly members that "victory" on this issue was not worth the risk of breaking up the UN, and that the U.S. Congress would certainly have refused to help pay for a UN peace-keeping operation which excluded our government from an important area, as the Soviet Union was convinced this operation had excluded it from the Congo.

An even more spectacular example of U.S. ambivalence

and self-righteousness about the UN was provided in 1971 by the Nixon Administration's handling of the Pakistan crisis. For many months we heedlessly refused to resort to UN machinery to compel General Yahya Khan to stop his genocide in East Pakistan which caused the exodus of ten million refugees into India; then, when India finally went to war, we piously denounced the UN for failing to do at the last minute what we had helped prevent it from doing in time.

The basic difficulty was that neither President Johnson nor President Nixon had any real respect for the United Nations. Both preferred to conduct their foreign affairs in the most unilateral and uninhibited manner they could get away with, and to resort to the UN only when they were reasonably certain it would support their position, or when they wished, as in the cases of Vietnam and Pakistan, to shift or share the blame for what had gone wrong. Even worse, by demanding that the United Nations do what it was not strong enough to do, or what a large majority of members were opposed to its doing, and then denouncing its failure to act, these Presidents seriously undermined among Congress and the public the steadfast U.S. support of the United Nations which is indispensable to its health and growth.

Another cause of the UN's decline since 1964 has been the breakdown of its peace-keeping in the Middle East. Thanks to Ralph Bunche and Dag Hammarskjöld, this had been the scene of some of its most brilliant successes between 1949 and 1967. The breakdown had two phases. The first was the precipitate withdrawal of the UN Emergency Force from the Sinai in May 1967, which made well-nigh certain the outbreak of war a fortnight later. Here the fault lay not with the UN or the Secretary General, but with the weakness of the ad hoc peace-keeping procedures which had been improvised when the great powers were unable to agree on the implementation of Article 43. Since under these ad hoc procedures a peace-keeping force could enter or remain in an area only with the consent of the host government, the UN Emergency Force had no alternative but to depart once Nasser withdrew his consent. Moreover, under the ad hoc procedures, the Force was composed of contingents voluntarily contributed by various governments which were free to recall them at any time, as in this case the Indian and Yugoslav governments did as soon as Nasser so requested. Therefore, being based on the consent of the states concerned rather than on a decision of the Security Council, the Force dissolved when that consent was withdrawn.

The second phase of the breakdown of peace-keeping in the Mideast began with the failure to implement the "peacemaking" resolution which the Security Council adopted with remarkable promptness on November 22, 1967. This resolution spelled out in broad terms the essential elements of a just and lasting peace in the Middle East. Yet five years later the Middle East seems as far as ever from such a peace, or indeed from any peace. Here again the fault lies not in the Charter itself but in the refusal of the members to enforce it. All those concerned sanctimoniously repeat that they would never think of "imposing" a settlement. Yet if the parties to a conflict demonstrate over a reasonable period of time that they are wholly unable to agree, and the absence of agreement seems almost certain to lead sooner or later to another serious breach of the peace, it is incumbent upon the Security Council under the Charter to "decide what measures shall be taken to maintain or restore international peace and security." In other words, it is the Council's solemn obligation under these circumstances either to impose a settlement—or at the very least to impose measures which will ensure that armed conflict is not renewed.

Finally, in all candor it must be admitted that the vast expansion in membership of the United Nations, from fifty-one in 1945 to a hundred and thirty-two in 1972, while essential to making it representative of the world as it actually is, has not enhanced the effectiveness of the institution. The problem derives from the fact that the UN *is* a reflection of the real world—that is, that the world today is arbitrarily and absurdly divided into more than a hundred and thirty sovereign independent nations, of which six have a population of over a hundred million but more than a quarter have a population of less than one million. This anomalous situation is accurately but counterproductively reflected in the United Nations.

It is frequently pointed out by critics of the UN that resolutions could be adopted by majorities in the General Assembly representing only about 10 percent of the world's population and about 5 percent of the UN's budget. In practice this never happens, but the fact that it theoretically could diminishes the credibility and prestige of the institution. What does happen is that an enormous amount of time is spent in profitless debate, and that the majority in the Assembly refuses to discipline itself by tightening up its procedures, lest the precious freedom of interminable speech for garrulous delegates be inhibited. Both the real and the symbolic defects of the Assembly would be compounded if a substantial additional number of "ministates" are admitted in the future.

It is usually forgotten by critics that the Assembly can take no binding decisions (except in regard to the UN's budget), that all its other resolutions are only recommendations and that binding enforcement action can be taken only by the Security Council. Nevertheless, the multiplication of small states in the organization has paradoxically increased, particularly among great powers, both skepticism about its effectiveness and apprehension about its pretensions. One might facetiously paraphrase Churchill to say that rarely have so few feared so much from so many.

I cannot end this brief review of what has gone wrong with the United Nations during the past few years without emphasizing again that the fault lies not with the organization itself but with its members, particularly the big powers, who are the five permanent members of the Security Council. Unlike sovereign governments, the United Nations has absolutely no independent authority of its own. No UN body—the Security Council, the General Assembly, the Economic and Social Council or any other—can decide any action or make any recommendation unless a qualified majority of the membership of that body has agreed to do so. In the case of the Security Council this means that all five permanent members must have agreed to the action, or at least have acquiesced to the point of not exercising their veto. The Secretary General has no authority to act outside of his own Secretariat except at the behest and under the instructions of one of these representative bodies. Therefore, when governments, the press or the public blame the United Nations for acting or failing to act in certain circumstances, they are either deceiving themselves or trying to deceive others. The responsibility for acting or failing to act rests directly and wholly on the member governments themselves.

The final section of this book will set forth recommendations for concrete reinforcement of United Nations machinery. First, however, I would like to make a few remarks about the United States Mission to the United Nations, the instrument by which our government conducts such secondary aspects of its foreign policy as it chooses or is obliged to carry on through this international organization. It was my pleasure and privilege to serve in this Mission as a deputy to Adlai Stevenson and later to Arthur Goldberg from 1961 to 1966, and as its chief from January 1969 to February 1971.

There has been considerable debate as to whether the Ambassador to the United Nations should be a prestigious political figure, such as Henry Cabot Lodge or Adlai Stevenson, or a career diplomat as I was and as are most of the representatives of other nations. Before I myself served as ambassador, I felt that the post should go to a prestigious political figure, and after serving in the position for two years I am confirmed in that opinion. It is true that an experienced diplomat can probably operate more effectively than a domestic politician inside the incredibly complicated labyrinth of the UN itself. What is even more important, however, is that he be able to operate effectively in the equally complicated labyrinth of Washington. If he has not the political prestige and steady access to the President, Secretary of State and leaders of Congress necessary to gain and hold their support for a UN-oriented foreign policy, he cannot be substantively effective at the UN, no matter how skilled a diplomat he may be. It is far better that he have the necessary "clout" in Washington and that he rely on experienced deputies and staff to guide him through the intricacies of the United Nations.

However, it has become all too clear in recent years that even the most prestigious and gifted political figures in this position are unable to play more than a limited part in the formulation of policy in Washington, even in policy vitally affecting U.S. interests in the United Nations. This seems to be true without much regard either to the formal status of the incumbent in the bureaucracy or to the political power he may have wielded before he occupied this position.

Those who have occupied the position are: Edward Stettinius, Jr., a former Secretary of State; Warren Austin, a former senator; Herschel Johnson, a career diplomat; Henry Cabot Lodge, a former senator; James Wadsworth, with a long career in government; Adlai Stevenson, twice Democratic nominee for the Presidency; Arthur J. Goldberg, a former Secretary of Labor and Justice of the Supreme Court; George Ball, a former Undersecretary of State; Russell Wiggins, former editor of the *Washington Post;* Charles Yost, a career diplomat; and George Bush, a former Congressman. On the whole one cannot complain of the quality of the appointments. President Eisenhower went so far as to make his appointee, Henry Cabot Lodge, a member of his Cabinet, and that practice has been continued by his successors.

Still, there has been far more shadow than substance to these often spectacular appointments and arrangements, at least during the ten years of my experience. Membership in the Cabinet has not proved to be of more than symbolic significance. Under recent Presidents the Cabinet as a body has been little involved in policy formulation, and almost never in *foreign*-policy formulation. In this respect, participation in meetings of the National Security Council is far more important to an Ambassador to the United Nations. In that capacity I was invited to take part in the consideration only of issues in which the UN was already deeply and inescapably involved, such as the Middle East and Southern Africa, but never in the broad range of other issues in which the UN could and often should have been involved.

However, the experience of two such personalities as Adlai Stevenson and Arthur Goldberg demonstrated how difficult it is for *any* Ambassador to the UN to play a decisive role in the Washington hierarchy. Both were men of very great prestige and ability; both had independent constituencies, one in the Democratic Party, the other in the labor movement; both had easy access to the Presidents under whom they served and had received solemn assurances from them about the role they could expect to play in the formulation and conduct of policy; both made a particular effort to work in harmony with the Secretary and Department of State and on the whole were successful in doing so. Yet one may fairly say that the power of both diminished steadily in Washington from the day they took office in New York.

Of course, there were special circumstances in each case. The bent of mind of Kennedy differed radically from that of Stevenson. They had great difficulty communicating with, not to mention understanding, each other. This difference of temperament and outlook was even more profound between Stevenson and Johnson. Johnson's policies, particularly in regard to Vietnam and the Dominican Republic, were often antipathetic to Stevenson, though he was obliged to defend them in the United Nations, and Johnson's habits of making policy through a tight group of four or five systematically excluded Stevenson from the center of power. Before he died he was bitterly disheartened and disillusioned with almost all aspects of his UN role.

I have the impression that Arthur Goldberg came to the UN with even more categorical assurances of the position he would hold and the part he would play, particularly in regard to Vietnam. However, when his views on that critical issue diverged from those of the President, as they soon did, his influence dwindled rapidly and his frustrations multiplied.

As to my own experience, it was quite clear to me from the outset that President Nixon, while he made all the proper noises publicly and privately about his commitment to the United Nations, and while he was quite prepared to help it play a larger role in economic development and protection of the environment, wanted no nonsense from it concerning the political and security issues on which the fate of his country and the world depends. These—Vietnam, arms limitation, European security, the Middle East, finance and trade and all the other ingredients of the balance of power—he intended to deal with in the traditional pre-World War II fashion: that is, either unilaterally or in direct negotiations with other powers and superpowers.

Therefore I had no illusions that though I was chosen not only as a career diplomat but as a Democrat, in order to give a bipartisan flavor to the appointment, I would have the political weight in either capacity to exercise a decisive influence on policy—or indeed that I would not be dropped whenever it became politically expedient to do so. Being a profound believer in the United Nations, I accepted the offer because I welcomed the opportunity to do what I could for it and because I suspected that if I did not, someone less committed to the institution, someone more accurately reflecting the Administration's lack of concern for it, would be chosen.

The usual assurances of faithful support and ready access to their persons were extended me by the President and Dr. Kissinger, but these rapidly became muted as more urgent matters occupied their minds. I do not recall that either of them ever asked my advice on any subject, though I took it upon myself to submit my views constantly and candidly in writing and, whenever I had the opportunity, at NSC and other meetings. On the other hand, my relations with Secretary of State Rogers and his principal assistants were close and cordial, my views on matters within my competence were regularly sought and presented, and at least in some cases these views prevailed.

While I am not familiar in detail with the relations of my successor, George Bush, with the White House, he has the advantage of being an ardent and active Republican and, I understand, a favorite of the President's. Still, these assets do not seem, as far as one can judge from outside, to have given him any substantial voice in policy-making in Washington, or even to avoid being obliged by the Administration to undertake foolish and impossible assignments at the United Nations on several occasions. Conspicuous among these were the effort to keep Taiwan in—and hence Communist China out—at the very moment Dr. Kissinger was in Peking arranging the President's visit there, and the effort to prevent war between India and Pakistan at the last minute after the causes of war had been allowed to accumulate unheeded for eight months. Perhaps Ambassador Bush has found, as Stevenson and Goldberg found before him, that even a significant position in the domestic political hierarchy does not assure a UN Ambassador anything approaching a decisive voice in Washington.

In part this deficiency of power results from the mere fact that an Ambassador to the UN must be absent from Washington most of the time and that, as most ambassadors overseas have found, *"les absents ont toujours tort"*—the absent are always wrong. The real problem, however, could not be overcome by any administrative arrangement or accommodation. The tragic and, so far, decisive fact is that the U.S. government, like the governments of the other strongest nations, is not yet convinced that its major interests will be best served by being dealt with in and through the United Nations. Our Ambassador there will not be at the center of power in Washington until the United Nations is more nearly at the center of power in world affairs.

It is to this paramount theme that I now turn in conclusion.

IV
An Agreed Concept
of Order

In a book published at the beginning of 1969, just before he assumed his duties as President Nixon's National Security Adviser, Henry Kissinger wrote: "The greatest need of the contemporary international system is an agreed concept of order."* There can be little doubt that this is true.

Since he became the President's adviser, Dr. Kissinger presumably has been trying to build his concept of order into peaceful relations among great powers, on which it most depends. I should not criticize his achievement, which is perhaps as much as one man could be expected to do in four short years. What I would criticize is his concept of order. It seems to me to be wholly insufficient to meet the modern need, to be backward rather than

*Henry Kissinger, *American Foreign Policy: Three Essays* (New York: W. W. Norton, 1969).

forward-looking, to be a vain attempt to use Metternich's nineteenth-century balance of power to stabilize an international "system" eroded and outmoded by twentieth-century technology. The "system" needs not only an *agreed* concept of order; it needs a wholly *new* concept of order. Otherwise we shall merely confirm René Grousset's judgment that all we can learn from history is that we don't learn from history.

In reflecting on prospects for the 1970's and 1980's, one conclusion seems to me inescapable: a qualitative change in the character of both human and international relations has been imposed by science and technology. Time and space have been prodigiously contracted, so that crises within societies and confrontations between them, which throughout human history have been cushioned by oceans and years, now explode in the briefest span of time and are at once echoed almost everywhere. In the poet's words, there is no longer "world enough and time" to make the leisurely correction of past errors and the haphazard adjustment to new conditions which have been customary in the past. Tomorrow is confounded pell-mell with today. The importunate future wakes us breathless each morning. Time no longer works in our favor. The situation does not ripen; it rots.

In terms of international relations, it should be clear that the new conditions created by science during the past thirty years can no longer be successfully met by traditional methods for the conduct of foreign affairs among nation-states. Nuclear weapons are far from safe in the hands of five; they would be uncontrollable in the hands of one hundred. Yet the doctrine of the sovereign equality of nations affords no solid basis for discrimination between the five and the one hundred. The multiplication of human beings—their insatiable appetite for resources and elbowroom, their generation of wastes and debris, their violent response to confinement or conglomeration—will no longer permit the license of an uncurbed birth rate. Now that technology has spoiled its rationalization, the coexistence of affluence and misery cannot provide a basis for international security any more than it can for national health.

These are but three examples among many which demonstrate that in the conditions of the last quarter of the twentieth century even the traditional objects of foreign policy—national security, avoidance of major war, mutually profitable commercial exchanges—are unlikely to be attainable by the old (that is, current) methods. Changes as profound, as qualitative and as rapid as those which have occurred in science and technology will soon be required in the conduct of relations among nations and people.

Of course, these changes will be enormously difficult to carry out. Over the past century men and women have cheerfully, even casually, adjusted their ways of life in many fundamental respects, but they are still disposed to resist desperately any change in their fundamental beliefs, no matter how anachronistic these may be. Doctrines still passionately clung to by millions of people —Marxism, so-called free enterprise, unrestricted national sovereignty—in practice have been partly superseded even where they are most piously acclaimed. Yet human beings can still be persuaded to die for them in large numbers.

Much of the fault lies with the leaders. In dictatorships they find it easier to rely on the bureaucratized parties or the military officer corps, which have brought them to power, than to risk innovations which, by shaking up the structure, might topple them from its summit. In democracies, leaders find it easier to campaign on old shibboleths and shopworn promises, fears of foreign devils and dreams of painless prosperity than to risk offending naïve majorities by telling them what they desperately need to know. Such leaders confront the breakdown of traditional standards by improvising moralities—and then moralize about the improvisations.

If civilization is to survive this century, there has to be a quantum jump in the exposure of the common man—whose century it was supposed to be—to the facts of life as he and his children will have to confront them in ten or twenty years. Otherwise, belatedly awakened from his dreams into a weird and incredible world, he will be as ill-equipped to cope with it as a naked man dropped on the moon.

Besides new beliefs, new institutions are required and will have to be created. Obviously we must begin with what we have and mold it as rapidly as we can into what it needs to become. Everything cannot be done at once. The world cannot be turned upside down without losing its head as well as its footing. Overnight revolutions are surprisingly unproductive. They are like those toy figures weighted at the bottom that always bob up into the same position no matter how completely one tips them over. As Robert Frost remarked, "Revolutions are one thing that should be done by halves." Industrial society requires and imposes more change than previous societies, but it also needs the past even more than they did. It is threatened with dissolution because it has changed too much and not enough—indiscriminately.

The remainder of this chapter is devoted to projecting over the next decade four parallel elements necessary for a more rational conduct of foreign affairs. In a properly balanced strategy all four should be pursued simultaneously, but those which are most significant now and in the immediate future may, if we move with the times, soon become secondary and eventually vestigial. On the other hand, those now only beginning to take shape may eventually occupy the whole spectrum, absorbing and consuming in their relevance to the future all the grandiose strategies and *raisons d'état,* which have distinguished the era of nation-states at such great cost to mankind.

National Honor and
National Interest

The aspect of the conduct of foreign affairs which most immediately needs improvement, because it is the most relevant to current practice, is the management of such affairs by separate national governments, along the lines discussed in earlier pages. Simply because it is still so predominant and yet so anachronistic, it is precisely this aspect that most urgently requires radical reform.

The phrase "national honor and national interest" is used here with a degree of irony. It has been employed in the past with a minimum of rigor and a maximum of vanity. National honor has been held to have been flouted when an ambassador is swatted with a fly whisk, or when an armed force recklessly and needlessly thrust into an exposed position is attacked. National interest is said to be involved when an ally, no matter how foolishly chosen, is overthrown or threatened, or when a private investment, no matter how acquired or who profits from it, is nationalized by a foreign government.

It is high time that these terms be defined both more realistically and more morally. Should Americans not consider that their national honor has been affronted when American soldiers massacre a community of innocent peasants, or when American airmen wipe out a village without knowing whether it shelters foe or friend? Should not Russians consider that their national honor has been violated when their government invades an allied country, throws out its government and persecutes those who supported it? Is it really so vital to the interest of the American people which nation or faction wins in Southeast Asia, the Middle East or the Indian subcontinent that the United States must be politically or even militarily involved there year after year? Is it really in the vital interest of the Soviet people that they build a great fleet to

sail the seven seas and inject themselves into the quarrels
of Arabs and Indians?

Before everything else, the leaders of nations and plan-
ners of national strategy need to change their preoccupa-
tions with these basic matters and to learn more down-
to-earth, commonsensical and humane responses to the
elementary questions they raise. They need to recall Alan
Paton's question, "In what way can one's highest loyalty
be given to one's country?" And his reply: "Surely only in
one way, and that is when one wishes with all one's heart
and tries with all one's powers, to make it a better country,
to make it more just and more tolerant and more merciful,
and if it is powerful, more wise in the use of its power."*

On the same level, leaders of peoples need to learn—as
American leaders are now being obliged to learn, but for
how long?—that they must reorder their priorities so that
the lion's share of available resources, which are limited
even in the richest states, may be devoted to the public
welfare in the most fundamental sense: sufficient food,
decent housing, impartial education, an expanding culture, a habitable environment, correction of crime, elimination of poverty. It is true that unless a nation can be
defended against external attack nothing it has is secure. It
is also true, however, that a nation is strong over the long
run only to the extent that it is internally united, confident
and progressive. Throughout history far more nations and
civilizations have succumbed to external attack because
they failed to cope with internal problems than because
they failed to arm themselves sufficiently. As Alfred North
Whitehead said, "Those societies which cannot combine
reverence to their symbols with freedom of revision must
ultimately decay."

Where a nation needs most to be strong in a real and
lasting sense is in its spirit. What its political and intellec-

*Quoted in *The New York Times,* June 18, 1971.

tual leaders should seek most to supply is inspiration, integrity and coherence, most of all, a sense of purpose aimed not at glory, conquest or the propagation of any faith, but at the establishment of a society so organized and so conducting itself that it will have tranquillity at home and respect abroad. That is not impossible in this age; the Scandinavian states meet those criteria. Is it necessary for a nation to be small in order to be rational or virtuous?

In general terms these are the qualities which should characterize the style and conduct of a nation-state and its leaders in these critical last decades of the twentieth century. I do not think they can be achieved among enough states quickly enough to make our present system safe and viable in time. If I am right, it follows that we must before long surpass it. However, as long as nation-states remain the chosen instrument of most of mankind, we must use their antiquated machinery as best we may, with as little recklessness, arrogance and self-righteous-ness as we can manage, with as much sophistication, sweet reason and humanity as we can muster. The means for better applying these principles to the current conduct of foreign affairs by separate national governments have been discussed throughout this book. In the few pages remaining I wish to concentrate on their more effective application through varying degrees of association among nations.

An Association
of Developed Democracies

Over the past quarter century, many in the West have contended that the world can be effectively managed and made secure only by an alliance or close association of the economically developed democracies of Western Europe,

North America and Japan. According to this thesis, the
Communist great powers are inveterately hostile and
aggressive whenever opportunity offers; the poor nations
of Asia, Africa and Latin America will be incapable of
self-sustaining growth, political stability or consistent
cooperation among themselves for many years; and the
United Nations, a flabby mix of all these incongruous
elements, can never do more than gabble and flounder.

On the other hand, the North Atlantic Treaty Organization has kept the peace in Europe for two decades and the
European Economic Community may soon become the
fourth or fifth great power. The Organization for Economic Cooperation and Development and the Group of Ten,
which represent the developed democracies, have been
reasonably effective in coordinating both their own financial and commercial relations and their joint or parallel
assistance to developing countries. At the same time,
private multinational cooperations, operating primarily in
developed states, multiply their joint capacities and draw
tighter the bonds between them. This record of achievement is an extraordinary one—indeed, one rarely encountered in history. Not only the West but the world
owes a debt of gratitude to Truman, Marshall, Acheson,
Monnet, Schuman, Bevin, Adenauer, Spaak, Pearson,
Heath and all the rest responsible for undertaking and
maintaining it.

It is not at all implausible that over the next decade or
two some more formal association of the developed democracies may emerge and become the predominant factor in global international relations. Certainly, from an
American point of view such an eventuality would not be
unattractive. Even discounting our natural bias in this
direction, one must grant that the main elements of
"civilization" during the past two hundred years, whether
technological, political or cultural, have been generated in
the "North Atlantic area"; only there, in Japan and in a
very few other countries have these elements been assimi-

lated and fused into a relatively stable society. From these peoples, therefore, one can most reasonably anticipate the enlightened leadership to enable the world as a whole to surmount the tensions, displacements and disruptions it confronts at the end of the twentieth century.

This said, however, one must add a series of caveats and reservations. First, for the leadership of these peoples to be effective, their association will have to become much more consistent, reliable and comprehensive than it has hitherto been. For Western Europe itself the so-called "Community" has not even become a full economic union. Politically, in the Gaullist tradition its component states continue to act far more often separately than jointly. The prospects for the early consolidation of a great power called "Europe" are still highly dubious.

Except in regard to East–West confrontations in Europe itself, the United States, the so-called "leader of the Free World," still prefers to move as a superpower in solitary and imperial grandeur, often in only perfunctory consultation with its principal allies. As recently as 1971 the Nixon Administration blandly confronted Japan and Western Europe with a series of momentous *faits accomplis* on matters of the greatest significance to them. Thus, while most Western leaders pay lip service to cooperation among the developed democracies, those enjoying the heady wine of office usually find it more exhilarating to act without the inhibitions which genuine and structured association require. Yet without such association there can be no Western leadership in a consistent and decisive sense.

Moreover, even if formal association or union among the developed democracies should eventually be achieved, it would be open to other hazards. If the more morbid tendencies in the nation-state system persist, it could merely lead to an Orwellian global confrontation of super superpowers—the West vs. Russia vs. China—each multiplying its nuclear arsenal in terror of the others, each striving to win or preempt an expanding empire in the Third World, each moving internally toward more rigorous totalitarianism in order better to confront the foreign foe.

Another unattractive but not implausible scenario would find a union of developed democracies, having negotiated a de facto standoff with the Communist powers, becoming in effect a "rich man's club," which seeks to insulate itself as much as possible from the hopeless problems and disorders of the remainder of mankind. But over the long run it is extremely doubtful that the developed democracies would be any more successful than the Romans were in ignoring or excluding the accumulating hordes of "barbarians," or that they would not sooner or later succumb to the same diseases which they had allowed to poison the societies outside their walls.

A far firmer association of the developed democracies is devoutly to be desired. Certainly a main objective of U.S. foreign policy in its present context should be not merely to preserve what already exists but substantially to strengthen the international monetary and trading systems, for the health of which these nations are because of their affluence most responsible. The ultimate objective should be a "common market" among them—certainly not an exclusive one, but one which would offer preferential treatment to developing nations and reciprocity to the Communist states.

Lest we become prematurely euphoric about such sensible conceptions, it must be reiterated that a closer association among developed democracies is still far from being achieved—and may never be. It is also necessary to emphasize that even if it were, only the most far-sighted and dispassionate leadership within it could prevent it from slipping into the conventional orbit of empires, and from suffering the fate all such empires have suffered in the past. If civilization is to be saved in the time available to us, something more solid, more comprehensive and more original than even an imperial league of democracies is required.

Peaceful Collaboration among Superpowers

It is a regrettable but inescapable fact that the United States and other developed democracies will have to continue to share this shrinking planet with the two Communist great powers; that hostile competition with them capable of generating an ultimate disaster is likely to remain the course of least resistance; and that neither side will be able to subdue or suppress the other without courting that disaster. In light of this, what the Communists have called "peaceful coexistence" between the two social systems would seem to be no more than the most elementary common sense. Indeed, their tedious confrontation might usefully be developed into something a little less neutral and separate than mere "coexistence," for, after all, they have a substantial common interest not only in survival but in a more temperate and congenial climate in their relationships.

However, this appreciation does not lead to the conclusion that a "Concert" of two, three or five great powers, including one or both of the Communists, is capable now or in the foreseeable future of stage-managing the world. In the first place, for the foreseeable future the differences between the traditions, philosophies, bureaucracies and objectives of East and West are too great to permit them to carry out common policies except in special cases. Secondly, an attempt by a few superstates, no matter how powerful, to dictate to the rest of the world would arouse the most intense and stubborn opposition. It is a characteristic myopia of leaders and theoreticians of superpowers to see the world in bipolar or tripolar terms, disregarding all the other nations and peoples less fortunately circumstanced or less centrally disciplined. Neither circumstances nor discipline can be counted on to endure through the vicissitudes of the coming decades.

Nevertheless, there is much short of "Concert" that the adversary great powers can do about their own relations that will make life more tolerable and secure for themselves and others. Far and away the most significant and sensible would be vastly to scale down their competition in arms. They have been talking about disarmament for twenty-five years, but it almost seems as though the more they talk the more they build. Despite interminable SALT and Geneva conferences, and some significant and promising agreements, the megatonnage of nuclear weapons and the profusion of conventional weapons continue to expand astronomically.

In my judgment, there is no convincing military reason why the following additional measures of nuclear disarmament should not now be proposed by the United States: an end to all nuclear testing, underground as well as in other environments; a rapid phasing out of all land-based intercontinental missiles; a rapid phasing out of the relatively few ABM's already constructed; a phasing out of bombing aircraft designed to carry nuclear weapons across oceans; an agreed limitation on the numbers of sea-based intercontinental missiles; a drastic reduction and subsequent limitation in the numbers of tactical nuclear weapons deployed; a regular exchange of information on research and development of new nuclear weapons and significant modifications in old ones. These proposals, if accepted—which they obviously could not be without long and painful negotiation—would essentially restrict the nuclear armament of the superpowers to limited numbers of sea-based ICBM's and of tactical weapons. Since there is no present or foreseeable threat to the invulnerability of sea-based missiles, these should be sufficient to deter attack and, if attack should occur, to provide assured retaliation. There is no military need for any more nuclear weapons than these, and there is an urgent political and economic need to do away with every weapon that is not vital militarily.

The United States, the Soviet Union and their respective allies in Europe also have every reason to negotiate a more substantial détente in Europe. Willy Brandt's policy of conciliation and the Soviet response to it have already laid the basis for such a détente, but so far all that has been done is to recognize formally that the territorial and political status quo exists and that neither side intends to change it. Here again the next needed step is in the military field. The confrontation of large armies in the center of Europe twenty-seven years after the end of the war is an absurdity. Brezhnev has no intention of marching to the English Channel, nor does Nixon of rolling back the Iron Curtain. Berlin has been guaranteed as much as its geographic position will ever permit it to be.

The forces on both sides—not just on ours—should be scaled down substantially at once, and progressively more and more. Admittedly, problems of this kind are rarely what they seem to be. The main reason the Soviets keep large numbers of troops in Eastern Europe is not for defense against the West but to deter and, if necessary, to suppress insubordination among their own allies—East Germany, Poland, Czechoslovakia, Hungary. The main reason Western Europe wants American troops in Germany is not to fight a war they do not expect but to maintain a visible equilibrium in a Europe unbalanced by Western fragmentation and Eastern centralization. These underlying realities cannot be easily ignored or circumvented, but they will not last forever. The West is gradually consolidating, the East diversifying. If a European security conference is held in 1973, as is proposed, its first purpose should be to commence the reduction of the redundant armies confronting each other so long, so provocatively and so unnecessarily.

A more comprehensive and less seriously explored area of accommodation between the United States and the USSR should deal with their competitive intrusions into the Third World, whether in the Mediterranean, the Middle East, Southeast Asia, the Indian Ocean, Africa or Latin America. These intrusions are dangerous to the two superpowers themselves, dangerous to their allies and, despite superficial appearances to the contrary, most dangerous of all to the nations armed and encouraged by their "protectors." Grudging experiments in accommodation have been made: the tacit delineation of "spheres of influence" in most of Eastern Europe and Latin America; consultation and the exercise of some restraint in the Middle East; offers to negotiate "parity of presence" in the Indian Ocean. Such efforts should be continued and intensified, but they are radically insufficient. What are needed are not expanding "spheres of influence" but expanding "spheres of abstention" (to use Lincoln Bloomfield's felicitous phrase)—that is, commitments such as some of the riparian states of the Indian Ocean have sought in the UN General Assembly that this area be preserved from external intrusion as a "zone of peace."

What are also needed are agreements to limit and reduce the outpouring of conventional arms to friendly states in which both superpowers so extravagantly indulge. Despite appearances to the contrary, these armaments are no more beneficial to either recipient or donor than are the competitive intrusions mentioned above. The flow of arms wastes the resources of the recipients and escalates the conflicts in which they are involved. It increases the dependence of recipient and donor on each other, and commits the donor to conflicts not of his own making and beyond his effective control. As noted earlier, the eventual result is sometimes to give a weak client the power to decide whether a strong patron is drawn into direct confrontation or even war.

When President Nixon came to office in January 1969 he promised to turn from an era of confrontation to an era of negotiation, and he has clearly tried to do so. However, as Henry Owen of the Brookings Institution pointed out three years later, "The era of confrontation is not giving way to the era of negotiation; the two are proving to be one and the same."*

Certainly there are times when one has the impression that the aim of both sides is negotiation, not settlement, for the obvious reason that negotiation itself achieves some measure of détente without requiring the hard decisions and painful concessions which settlement does. Yet even to maintain détente, negotiation must produce some results more often than at four-year intervals. Fortunately, there were important, though only preliminary, agreements at the Moscow summit in May 1972. To accelerate negotiation, there should be U.S.–Soviet summit meetings approximately once a year. Under these circumstances leaders would have a more personal compulsion to produce results. However, I would recommend that these meetings take place in a more multilateral context, preferably the United Nations.

It is extremely interesting to note that recently a senior Soviet official of the UN Secretariat, Evgeny Chossudovsky (and Soviet officials even in the UN do not often speak without authorization), has publicly suggested that the concept of "peaceful coexistence" be fleshed out "by an institutional mechanism providing on a continuing basis the means for specific undertakings for the maintenance of peace and security. . . . A general framework could be sought in appropriate regional arrangements (such as a Treaty Organization for European Security and Cooperation) related to the United Nations, the world body where the several coexistence efforts might ultimately coalesce . . . . At some point in time, it would seem, a major policy decision will have to be made by all concerned to explore the modalities of a lasting collaborative arrangement be-

The Washington Post, January 12, 1972.

tween the West and the East. . . . There has rarely been a more propitious time than now when inescapable economic and social imperatives call for a new political impetus."*

These are valuable and pregnant suggestions, particularly the proposal indicating the United Nations as the body "where the several coexistence efforts might ultimately coalesce." I should myself strike out the word "ultimately." No mere concert of big states, especially one which is half democratic and half authoritarian, can by itself control conflicts, except possibly its own. What is needed are not merely self-denying ordinances from the great powers, desirable as these would be, but impartial, effective international machinery for dealing with any conflict that threatens international peace and security. This is precisely what the United Nations was created to be and what the great powers could make it at any time if they so desired. There, inside the framework of embryonic international institutions, is the area of great-power accommodation which would be safest and surest both for containing current conflicts and for building the foundations of a new world order.

To sum up, what is most immediately required for a more rational conduct of foreign affairs falls within the traditional framework: first, by national governments, a reappraisal of their basic concepts, a reordering of their goals and a more efficient management of their machinery; second, a much closer association among the developed democracies, together with a just and generous exercise of leadership on their part; third, a much bolder effort by the adversary great powers to reduce dangerous competition between them, particularly in nuclear armaments and inside the Third World.

All these endeavors should proceed vigorously and concurrently. However, none of them, or all of them

*Foreign Affairs, April 1972.

together, will prove to be more than palliatives in coping with the formidable complex of new crises confronting mankind. Far more radical and comprehensive action among nations is required during the next two decades if human civilization as it has evolved over the past thousand years is to be preserved.

United Regions and United Nations

The domestic history of France from Louis XI to Louis XIV, a period of about two hundred years, largely revolved around the struggle between the king and the great nobles—that is, around the consolidation of vast quasi-autonomous feudal domains into a single national state. The same process has taken place in many other parts of the world in varying ways but to much the same end. In Russia it was achieved by the Romanovs, most of all by Peter the Great. In India it was carried out by the British, who re-created the empire of the Moguls. In the United States it was accomplished in happier circumstances in the two decades before Washington's inauguration. In China, after a century of breakdown, the Communists reestablished the unity of the Celestial Kingdom. In Europe it seems possible that the 1970's may witness the peaceful creation of the first quasi-continental union there since the Holy Roman Empire.

There seems no reason to believe that a pattern of consolidation and unification of larger and larger territorial entities, which has been going on for five hundred years, should be arrested at this present incongruous stage, or that there is anything sacred or admirable about the contemporary division of the world into four or five vast units and more than a hundred small ones. No doubt some old nations will still break up and some new ones still appear; possibly we are all doomed to the same disintegration and anarchy that ended the Roman Empire; but there seems a better chance that technological imperatives, which were lacking in the Roman age, will prevail in this one.

Probably political consolidation will continue, but there are two pertinent and fundamental questions about the process. First, will it go through a stage of organization by continental or transcontinental regions, some perhaps dominated by one of the present great powers, others incorporating sufficient indigenous strength and coherence to constitute a new great power? In such a disposition one could imagine communities or commonwealths of Western Europe, Eastern Europe, North America, Latin America, Africa, East Asia, South Asia and Australasia. Some of the hazards of such a partial consolidation of the world into a few superpowers were suggested earlier in this chapter in the discussion of an association of developed democracies. One could easily imagine, for example, the same sort of crises and wars that are typical of our present international anarchy arising among these new superpowers over such borderlands as Yugoslavia, the Middle East, Nepal or Afghanistan, Southeast Asia or Taiwan, Cuba or Panama.

The second fundamental question about this process of supernational consolidation is whether, even if it takes place, it could proceed fast enough to stave off the foreseeable disasters flowing from our compulsive technology—nuclear weaponry, the radical discrepancy between death and birth control, the devastation of the biosphere by affluence, and the unmet expectations of the poor.

It has been the central thesis of this book that the nation-state system, which has served humanity reasonably well for several centuries, is now too parochial, too clumsy, too competitive and too unscrupulous to serve us safely any longer. Since most of mankind is still subject to its myths, however, it is unlikely to be replaced quickly.

The best we can hope for over the next couple of decades is a progressive ventilation and illumination of the public mind about the realities of the age in which we live; some far-reaching improvements in the operation of the present international "system," primarily along lines summarized in this chapter; and finally, a more intensive use of the international institutions already in being, which provide the most promising framework for eventual union.

The most congenial movement in the latter direction might be a further development of regional organizations. Nations are ambivalent about their neighbors. Often they hate and fear them more than states on the other side of the planet. Still, there is an underlying kinship and affinity even among traditionally hostile neighbors. A Frenchman and a German have more in common than either has with a Chinese. While far from identical, Latin Americans often have identical perceptions of the world. So do Africans. Hence it is not surprising that in recent times many of the first halting steps toward international consolidation have been within regional confines.

Significant progress in this sense has obviously been most notable in Western Europe, and to a much lesser degree in the so-called North Atlantic area, that is, Europe plus the United States and Canada. In the former, progress will certainly continue, though there is serious question as to how far it will go. Closer association in the North Atlantic area, if it occurs, seems likely to be less military than in the past, and to be dependent on overcoming the obstacles to more effective economic cooperation among the developed democracies.

Prospects seem much less favorable, at least in the near future, in other regions. So far, neither the Organization of American States, nor the Organization of African Unity, nor the Arab League, nor any of the even looser associations in East Asia, such as the Asian and Pacific Council, has been able to weld the disparate sovereignties, ideologies and interests of its members into an integrated instrument of common purpose. It is eminently desirable that they do so, and no doubt they will continue to try, particularly if the European effort proves to be a success. Certainly the United States should give every reasonable encouragement and support, as it has so wisely done in Western Europe and Latin America, to these movements toward regional consolidation.

My own impression, however, is that in most of these cases the difficulties of establishing close-knit, effective political and security institutions within regional bounds are almost as great as developing similar institutions on a global scale would be. Indeed, considering the imbalance of power in some regions, the difficulties and hazards may be even greater. Moreover, the risk of creating chauvinist supernationalisms in regional form is sufficiently great to make it unwise to disperse among separate regions the main responsibility for next steps in international consolidation. It would probably be just as practical—as well as more compatible with the ultimate aim—to place the main emphasis at once on the further reinforcement of already existing and already stronger global institutions.

By far the most important of these is the United Nations, its principal organs and its numerous family of agencies. Among the most significant of the latter are the International Monetary Fund, the International Bank, the UN Conference for Trade and Development, the UN Development Program, the World Health Organization, the Food and Agriculture Organization, the UN Educational, Scientific and Cultural Organization, the International Labor Organization, the International Atomic Energy Commission and the Conference of the Committee on Disarmament.

In the words of the Preamble to the Charter, the central purposes of the United Nations are "to save succeeding generations from the scourge of war," "to unite our strength to maintain international peace and security," "to establish conditions under which justice and respect for

. . . treaties and . . . international law can be maintained," "to promote social progress and better standards of life in larger freedom," "to reaffirm faith in fundamental human rights," and "to practice tolerance and live together in peace with one another as good neighbors." For these purposes certain specific but limited powers are conferred upon the principal organs of the United Nations, first of all binding the great powers on the Security Council to the maintenance of international peace and security. By adhering to the Charter, all member states have undertaken a solemn and binding commitment, in the words of Article 2 (2), to "fulfill in good faith the obligations assumed by them in accordance with the present Charter."

Sad to say a very large proportion of the member states, including all five permanent members of the Security Council, have repeatedly—one might almost say consistently—violated the Charter during the twenty-seven years since they signed it. One need only quote three of the principles set forth in Article 2 to which all members solemnly committed themselves: "All Members shall settle their international disputes by peaceful means in such a manner that international peace and security, and justice, are not endangered"; "All Members shall refrain in their international relations from the threat or use of force against the territorial integrity or political independence of any state"; "All Members shall give the United Nations every assistance in any action it takes in accordance with the present Charter."

International peace and security, not to mention justice, have repeatedly been endangered by the failure of the great powers to settle by peaceful means their disputes over Berlin, Korea, Cuba and Vietnam. It is true that general war was avoided in each case, but not through the machinery provided by the Charter and only at the brink, out of fear of mutual destruction. Israel and its Arab neighbors, India and Pakistan—both sets of antagonists backed by friendly big powers—have repeatedly refused to settle their disputes by peaceful means and have gone to war several times. Britain and France used force against the political independence of Egypt in 1956; the Soviet Union against that of Hungary in 1956 and of Czechoslovakia in 1968; the United States against that of Cuba in 1961 and of the Dominican Republic in 1965. A large number of members, including in each case one or more of the big powers, have refused to assist the United Nations in authorized peace-keeping actions in the Middle East, the Congo and Cyprus, and in embargoes imposed on Rhodesia, South Africa and Portugal.

None of these are failures of the United Nations. They are failures of the member states to carry out the obligations they have undertaken, to act together for the purposes they have laid down, and to use the international machinery for peace-keeping they themselves created.

What is required to make the United Nations an effective instrument for "harmonizing the actions of nations" and saving "succeeding generations from the scourge of war" is an act of will on the part of its strongest members to use it for exactly these purposes: to negotiate and settle disputes with their adversaries within rather than outside the UN framework; to rely on its instruments of conciliation and enforcement rather than on their own bilateral brawls and unilateral weaponry; to forestall or stop wars by interposing UN forces rather than injecting their own; and to insist that their friends and allies do likewise. The United Nations needs to be allowed to make decisions on issues affecting the peace of the world and to be enabled to enforce those decisions. Some of the machinery for doing so is already in place; the rest could be assembled within a short time. What is lacking is will.

Within the next decade or two, the great powers and the militarily or economically robust "middle powers" will face a fundamental choice: whether to conduct relations with each other in the traditional, uninhibited, competitive, militant manner, deepening an international anarchy incompatible with postindustrial society; or else to cushion their rivalries, seek their accommodations, and discipline peace-breakers within a universal and impartial organization. I am convinced that it will prove to be in the national interest of the great powers themselves to conduct more of their relations with each other and most of their relations with the Third World within the framework of the United Nations, where all are represented. It will be to their own interest to convey to the United Nations enough power and resources, military and financial, to control conflicts which might otherwise be the occasion for fatal confrontations, and to rely almost exclusively for aid to the Third World on UN agencies—whose objective and multinational character will spare the great powers unhappy direct involvements.

Obviously all the problems of U.S. foreign policy, for example, cannot be laid in the lap of the UN. One immediate proposal to policy-makers in Washington might be that as each new problem arises or old one reappears, they first consider whether it could not best be dealt with through UN machinery—rather than, as is now usually the case, turning to the UN, often with tongue in cheek, only when all other means have been exhausted and war or disaster impends.

Equally obviously, the future utility of the UN for keeping the peace will also depend on the cooperation of the other permanent members of the Security Council—that is, on their likewise becoming persuaded that multilateral rather than unilateral response to most threats to the peace is less hazardous and costly to themselves. To date the Soviets have been far from persuaded of this fact. Since the Congo operation they have been so chary of giving the Secretary General any authority over peace-keeping that they have blocked all efforts to revive and enlarge the UN's capacities in this field. As recently as the conversation with Prime Minister Kosygin in July 1971 reported in the opening section of this book, he told his American interlocutors that "other nations" would be unwilling to see the UN act as "the world's gendarme." In fact, it is not primarily other nations that have been unwilling, but the Soviet Union itself. (However, it is interesting to note that in the initial exchange of toasts during the 1972 Moscow summit, while President Nixon did not refer at all to the United Nations, President Podgorny reminded him: "Under the United Nations Charter, the Soviet Union and the United States as permanent members of the Security Council are called upon to play an important role in maintaining international peace together with other members of the Security Council.")

A new complication has been created by the representation of the People's Republic of China on the Security Council. For reasons obviously arising from its own fears, it has been a staunch proponent of uninhibited national sovereignty and a strong opponent of any interference in the internal affairs of sovereign states. This posture could lead it to oppose any form of UN peace-keeping.

I suspect, however, that the attitude of the majority of the Third World, which both the Communist great powers are assiduously and competitively cultivating, will eventually determine their position on this question. If the principal nations of the Third World prefer to resort to foreign or civil war as the spirit moves them, seeking needed aid and comfort from friendly great powers to help them do so as lethally as possible, there will be little compulsion for the powerful states to allow the UN to be "the world's gendarme." But should most of the Third World countries come to the soberer conclusion (which, on the whole, characterized their attitude in the early 1960's) that their security and welfare can be more surely safeguarded by effective international machinery than by rival great powers, in time they may be able to persuade the great powers to strengthen and use such machinery.

Once again it comes down to a question of will, determination and conviction—the will on the part of the United States to assume the leadership in a persistent, intensive effort to enable the United Nations to do what we ourselves originally designed it to do; the determination on the part of the middle and smaller states not just to sit passively by, waiting for the big powers to agree, but actively to persuade, press and push the big powers into agreement on this issue; the consequent conviction on the part of the two Communist great powers that it is more in their interest to move with the tide of UN reinforcement than to continue to thwart it and maintain uncurbed an international anarchy whose consequences for themselves are unpredictable.

What precisely is required to enable the United Nations to do what it was designed to do, and neither more nor less? Though some would be useful, amendments to the Charter are not essential at this stage, and premature efforts to push them through would provoke more discord than agreement. What is first required is to make the Charter work as it stands.

I shall summarize briefly what needs most to be done.*

The central problem is "maintaining international peace and security." The Charter gave this responsibility to the Security Council, and that is where it should remain—as long as the Council is permitted to function. Resort to the General Assembly for this purpose is always possible and has proved effective in rare cases—for example, the Suez crisis of 1956. However, the Assembly is a cumbersome body of a hundred and thirty-two members; it has the power only to recommend, not to decide. It could make recommendations by a large majority over the opposition of all or most of the great powers, but in the security field such recommendations have been and clearly will continue to be futile. Normally, peace-keeping action should continue to be sought in the Security Council, where at

*For a fuller examination of this problem see *The United Nations in the 1970's*, a report by a policy panel of the United Nations Association of the United States, published in September 1971.

least the acquiescence of five great powers is required, and at least their neutrality, if not their cooperation, in carrying out the Council's decisions can be expected.

The veto is both the strength and weakness of the Council. It is its strength because the veto assures each of the great powers that the UN will not be mobilized against it, and that it will not be required to join in enforcement action of which it disapproves. It is also the Council's weakness because, if misused, it can frustrate action of any kind. It is not feasible to abolish the veto at this time, though it should be possible to gradually attenuate it. Agreements might eventually be reached to use it sparingly—for example, only when two or more permanent members wish to do so, or only when "enforcement action" by the UN is proposed. In the last analysis, however, effective action by the Council will depend on the willingness of the majority, including all its permanent members, to cooperate or at least not to obstruct. Whether that willingness exists will not be determined by the presence or absence of the right to veto.

Three other points should be made about the Council. The first is its membership. With some reason, Japan believes itself to be as fully entitled to permanent membership as China, Britain or France. The problem is that if membership in the exclusive "club of five" were thrown open, there would be several candidates—for example, India, Brazil, West Germany and Italy. If all the candidates were admitted, and a corresponding number of new nonpermanent members as well, the exercise of the veto would no doubt become more rather than less common, and the size of the Council would become unwieldy. Until a propitious time occurs to revise the Charter fundamentally, it seems more prudent to retain the present size of the Council but to elect frequently to nonpermanent membership such states as those listed above that are best fitted to play a major role in the maintenance of international security.

For that purpose what would be most desirable would be, after all these years, a successful negotiation of the agreements envisaged under Article 43 of the Charter, whereby members would "undertake to make available to the Security Council, on its call . . . , armed forces, assistance, and facilities" to deal with threats to and breaches of the peace. Until such comprehensive and binding agreements are feasible, the next best step would be a substantial reinforcement of the ad hoc peace-keeping procedures which worked reasonably well in the Congo, Cyprus and, for a time, in the Middle East. Negotiations with this end in view have been going on at the United Nations for seven years and could be successfully completed in a short time if the points long at issue between the United States and the USSR were resolved—and if China would agree. The central elements of these ad hoc procedures are earmarked contingents of national forces which governments would agree in advance to make available for peace-keeping operations at the request of the Security Council; and the establishment in advance of a modest emergency fund to pay for such operations, as well as commitments to contribute further funds as the need arises.

The most critical moot issue in this procedure is the extent to which countries involved in a conflict would have a veto on the dispatch of UN forces to their territory, or a right to demand the withdrawal of those forces at a later date without Security Council approval. If single states have this right, they can wholly frustrate UN peace-keeping and thereby jeopardize not only their own security but everyone else's. If single states do not have this right, the fifteen members of the Security Council and the nations contributing peace-keeping forces would indeed assume the responsibility of serving as the "world's gendarme." No one can venture to predict at this juncture just when the world may be ready for so significant a forward step. It could occur suddenly and unexpectedly, over a conflict so pregnant with potential disaster for everyone that no one, including the great powers, would dare leave its resolution to the passions and biases of the states directly involved. Such a situation would be precisely what the authors of the Charter contemplated and thought they had provided for.

If the Security Council is ever to be called upon to intervene by force in conflicts which have gotten out of hand and threaten the general peace, it would logically follow that it should first also involve itself more decisively in the settlement of disputes which, if unresolved, are likely to lead to conflicts of that magnitude. Therefore, it would seem proper—indeed, essential—that whenever the Security Council has been able to agree on a settlement which it considers just and necessary, it should have the authority to impose that settlement on the parties concerned. Admittedly, this, too, will be extremely difficult. It, too, involves a gross infringement of the "sacred principle" of unlimited national sovereignty. However, it also involves the choice between international law and order, on the one hand, and anarchy and war on the other. The Security Council, aided by the Secretary General, the International Court and the General Assembly, should do all in its power to assist and induce parties in a serious dispute or an impending conflict to agree among themselves. But if the parties will not agree, as a last resort the Council must be able to impose and enforce its own settlement. Otherwise the fate of hundreds of millions of people may be decided not by the highest and most responsible councils of mankind but by a few passionate men in a few bellicose capitals, just as much of the fate of this century was decided in Belgrade, Vienna and St. Petersburg in July 1914.

This is not the place to lay out elaborate proposals for the reform and invigoration of the United Nations, but I would like to touch on three more points. First, there is a serious danger that if many more so-called ministates are admitted as members, the growing popular impression that the UN is not representative of the real world will be accentuated, and its prestige will further decline. There should be established a new category of "associated states" which would enjoy the protection and support of the UN, as well as full access to it, but would neither pay dues nor vote.

Secondly, there should be a substantial reinforcement of the capacities of the most significant UN organs and agencies in the economic field—the Economic and Social Council, the Monetary Fund, the World Bank and the Development Program—to coordinate, orchestrate and expand economic relations among nations, in the areas both of trade and investment and of development and technical assistance. The necessary machinery is almost all in place; what is now needed is to give it more authority, more sophisticated refinement, more resources, and to replace some of the nuts and bolts that have become rusty from disuse.

Finally, a truly ridiculous impediment needs to be removed. Mankind's paramount instrument for survival, its only impartial and comprehensive institution for maintaining peace and security, runs a perennial financial deficit and is constantly on the verge of not being able to meet its payroll—so outrageously have governments (which spend each year $200 billion for a "defense" which each year leaves them more insecure) confused and ignored rational priorities. In terms of current national budgets, the deficit is microscopic: less than $200 million. The United States alone could wipe it out for the cost of about two days of the Vietnam war at its height. As it is, the total annual cost to the United States of all UN agencies is less than the annual cost of the New York City Fire Department. And yet there are members of Congress who are so petty or short-sighted as to wish to reduce these contributions even further. There should be no further delay in taking the necessary measures to clean up the deficit, to ensure a steady income for approved administrative purposes, to set up a modest "peace-keeping fund" to be available in emergencies, and to increase substantially contributions to the principal UN agencies engaged in economic development.

Even if all the steps which I have suggested were promptly taken, if the United Nations were restored by the states which created it to the central position in world affairs which they originally intended for it, it would still fall far short of being a world government or a world federation. It would remain what it is—a loose association of sovereign independent nations. But over and above the immediate benefits its member states would reap from a peace-making and peace-keeping organization so reformed and strengthened, their more intensive participation in it would eventually tend to create habits of collective action and closer association, an accumulating climate of receptivity to further development in this same direction. What would be the ultimate outcome no one knows. What can be said is that either the United Nations will evolve toward a much more integrated world, a true global federation of nations; or it will fall apart and be replaced by another, more successful experiment of the same kind; or, if neither happens, at some point in the next century there will be an almost total breakdown of both international and national society.

Our ultimate goal should be a world ordered and structured at least as well as the developed nations now are. There would have to be a federal charter, a federal authority, a central executive and parliament with overriding powers in those areas where the unrestricted license of one sovereignty could jeopardize the tranquillity and welfare of all sovereignties. Its main fields of competence might initially be limited to sufficient preponderant military power to prevent large-scale violence; the compulsory adjudication of disputes between states; the protection of the common environment from gross misuse and serious contamination; a central monetary system; a balanced trading system; organized, cooperative development of underdeveloped areas, including the high seas and sea-beds; the use of outer space; and the maintenance of public health and population balance.

Such a federal authority would in no way be incompatible with the widest administrative decentralization, with the most fertile diversity of culture and of religious, political and economic doctrine and practice. Indeed, minorities in existing states could safely be granted more autonomy, since the separation of sovereignties would be less marked and significant. All of us would tend to become "minorities" enjoying equal rights in a world society. The concepts of "foreigner" and "foreign affairs" would wither away and be replaced by a sense of common kinship and citizenship.

One successful model of such a federal system has long existed: the United States of America. Another, even more heterogeneously composed, may now be emerging in Europe. Significant elements of such a system are present in such diverse nations as the Soviet Union, India, China, Brazil and Nigeria. In fact, it would seem to follow the grain of history that all these unions, together with those peoples still accidentally disunited, might eventually merge into a single universal political structure, polymorphous and flexible but sufficiently integrated to preclude civil war and to cope with intolerable overloads of either affluence or deprivation.

Such a rational organization of human society is usually dismissed as Utopian. But as I once said in another book, what may come to seem Utopian in the perspective of history are the curious endeavors of most of our present leaders, inspired by a passionate and reckless nostalgia, to apply to emerging twenty-first-century circumstances the political, military and economic techniques of the nineteenth and early twentieth centuries. Most of those techniques worked badly even then. How can anyone suppose they can be made to work better, or at all, in an unimaginably different future?

A Last Word

If these prescriptions were followed, during the next decade or two there would take shape a composite system for the conduct of foreign affairs, a fabric of loosely interwoven strands in which those now most conspicuous would tend with time to unravel, while those now most frail would become stronger till finally they composed the whole cloth.

Customary bilateral relations among nation-states would continue more or less as in the past, though more wisdom, prudence and simple rectitude would be applied to their conduct. Adversary great powers would seek with somewhat more sincerity and boldness to lessen friction between themselves and to understand each other better. Developed democracies would maintain some institutions for their common welfare and defense, but would limit their military extravagance to the irreducible minimum necessary to balance the irreducible minimum of their adversaries. The Third World would be regarded not as an object for competition or preemption but as a partner in the common cultivation of law, abundance and brotherhood. The United Nations would be strengthened and used as the main instrument of peace-making and peace-keeping among nations, and would also serve as the elementary prototype, to be perfected over time, of an eventual world federation.

None of this may happen. It may prove beyond the capacity of retarded mankind to pry his loyalties loose from tribal totems, so long bathed in his blood. It may be beyond his wit to adapt his traditional national policies to the overriding new conditions described in the second chapter of this book. "Institutions, like technology," Philip Slater recently wrote, "are materializations of the fantasies of a past generation inflicted on the present."* Our present civilization, like that of the Greek city-states or the Roman Empire, may not have an imagination quick and supple enough to change its fantasies and institutions in time. Yet it could be the salvation of our children if world order, along with technology, were the fantasy which our generation "inflicted" on the future.

John Lukacs has said, "We live now amidst the ruins of civilization; but most of these ruins are in our own minds." If we could cleanse and elevate our minds, it would not be difficult to restore and transform our civilization. A quantum leap upward might take place if we could control and exploit the instruments of technology. If we cannot, they will devastate our civilization and leave nothing behind but ashes and barbarians—that is, ourselves.

The fact is that for the first time in history man has unlimited power for good or evil—that is, unlimited power over his own fate. But this power will be self-destructive unless he can purge his mind of old myths and reshape it to the curve of the future. If he can, anything is possible—even the rational conduct of those affairs which are still so foreign, often so frivolous and potentially so fatal.

*Philip Slater, *The Pursuit of Loneliness* (Boston: Beacon Press, 1970).

Index

About the Author

CHARLES W. YOST joined the U.S. Foreign Service in 1930 and was with it for more than thirty-five years. Among his many posts during this period, he served as ambassador to Laos, Syria and Morocco, as minister to Paris and as Deputy High Commissioner in Vienna. He was a member of the U.S. delegations at Dumbarton Oaks, the San Francisco conference which founded the United Nations, and the Potsdam Conference in 1945.

From 1961 to 1966 Mr. Yost was Deputy Representative to the United Nations. In January 1969 President Nixon appointed him Permanent Representative of the United States to the United Nations, and he held this position until his retirement in February 1971. In 1964 he was appointed Career Ambassador, the highest permanent rank in the Foreign Service.

In that same year Mr. Yost received a Rockefeller Public Service Award in recognition of his "sustained distinguished service to the United States in the field of Foreign Affairs." Today he is a lecturer in foreign policy at the Columbia University School of International Affairs, Counsellor to the United Nations Association, and a syndicated columnist for a number of daily newspapers.